The MASTER ARTIST WITHIN

The Art and Science of Redirecting Your Creative Energy

Expanded Edition

Teri Tompkins

The MASTER ARTIST WITHIN

The Art and Science of Redirecting Your Creative Energy

Expanded Edition

Copyright © 2018 Teri Tompkins

All rights reserved in all media under US and International Law. No part of this book may be copied or reproduced without written permission from the author.

Cover design by Brian Miller

Available on Amazon.com and other retail outlets.

Anastasia Publishing

ISBN: 0692139540

ISBN-13: 978-0692139547

Thank You for your help, love, editing, and encouragement during the creation of this book:

Rain Byars, Alicia Tompkins, Snowden McFall, Cindy Wilson, Jan Neff, Angel Harper, and all my artistic friends, heroes, and teachers.

CONTENTS

INTRODUCTION 1

- The Origin of The Master Artist Within Methodology 1
- A Word About Metaphor and Mythology 6

PART I

The Mystery of Creative Genius and Authenticity

1. WHO IS THE MASTER ARTIST WITHIN? 9

- 3 Qualities of Artistic Mastery 10
- Why Art? 11
- Creative Authenticity and the True Self 13
- Divine Inspiration for Heretics, Pagans, and Misfits 16
- Encouraging Artistic Mastery and Authenticity in Young People 17

2. THE "TWO WORLDS" OF CREATIVITY 21

- The Known World and the Unknown World 23

3. RECLAIMING AND REDIRECTING YOUR CREATIVE ENERGY 27

- The Illusion of Busy Work 29

4. FIRST, CREATE YOUR SECRET JOURNAL OR SKETCHBOOK 35

PART II

CREATIVE OBSTACLES: Understanding Creative Blocks, Limitations, and Challenges

5. RECOGNIZING CREATIVE OBSTACLES 41

- Fear, Pain, Confusion, and Other Dragons: 12 Types of Creative Obstacles 44
- The Empowerment of Owning Your Obstacles 45
- Transforming A Creative Challenge 46
- Dragon Mythology 46
- Using the Creative Obstacle Checklists 48

6. THE CREATIVE LIMITATIONS OF JUDGING AND BLAMING 51

7. LIMITING OPINIONS THAT SABOTAGE CREATIVITY 59

- Pleasing Clients and Patrons 61

8. CREATIVE CONFUSION 65

- Five Possible Sources of Creative Confusion 66

9. SECRET AGENDAS THAT LIMIT CREATIVITY 73

10. CONTROL AND MANIPULATION AS CREATIVE OBSTACLES 79

11. HABITS AND ADDICTIONS THAT BURDEN ARTISTS 85

- Habits Versus Addictions 91
- Understanding Motivations for Habits and Addictions 92
- Finding or Offering Help When Needed 94

12. THE SEA OF TRANSITION 99

- Transition Projects 100

13. SELF DOUBT AS AN ARTISTIC CHALLENGE 105

- Doubt Based on Past Failures 107

14. LIMITING BELIEFS THAT HIDE YOUR ARTISTIC GENIUS 113

- Hidden Beliefs 114
- Give Yourself Credit 114

15. CREATIVE SABOTAGE 121

- Self-Sabotage 123

16. THE MANY FACES OF FEAR 129

- From Fear to Enthusiasm 132

17. WHEN ARTISTS GO CRAZY 137

- Types of Crazy 138
- Help 144

PART III

FOUNDATION SKILLS AND TOOLS FOR THE ARTIST:
Transforming Creative Obstacles into Artistic Mastery and Authenticity

18. FOUNDATION SKILLS FOR CREATIVE MASTERY   149

Skill #1. **Take Excellent Care of The Artist**   150

Skill #2. **The Creative Power of Love and Kindness**   154

Skill #3. **Willingness**   156

Skill #4. **The Art of Paying Attention**   158

Skill #5. **The Importance of Movement**   161

Skill #6. **Practice Your Craft**   163

Skill #7. **Find Your Enthusiasm**   165

Skill #8. **A Healthy Sense of Humor**   166

Skill #9. **The Artist's Studio**   168

Skill #10. **Your Guiding Star**   169

19. TOOLS FOR THE ARTIST - AN INTRODUCTION   173

- 10 Techniques for Transforming Creative Obstacles   174

20. THE TRUE SELF/FALSE SELF GAME   177

- Instructions for the True Self / False Self Game   179
- The True Self / False Self Example Pages   181

21. THE ART OF FORGIVENESS   185

- Untying the Knots That Bind Us   187
- Tricky Situations   189

22. WRITING FOR CLARITY   193

- The Writing for Clarity Exercise   194
- Instructions for the Writing for Clarity Exercise   196

23. THE CIRCLE GAME   201

- Directions for the Circle Game   202
- The Circle Game Example Pages   204

24. SOUND AND FREQUENCY   207

- Suggestions for Using Sound and Frequency to Transcend Creative Difficulties   209

25. THE ART OF READING REFLECTIONS   213

- Mirrors   213
- Reflections Through Our Art   214
- Reflections Through Others   214
- Reflections of What We Love   215
- Transformation   216

26. THE ART OF LETTING GO   219

27. MEDITATION AS AN ART FORM   223

28. QUESTIONING FOR CLARITY   229

- Examples of Questions to Ask in the Studio   231

29. FOLLOWING THE TRAIL OF TRUTH   235

References and Notes   241

Image Notes   248

About the author   251

Detail of Michelangelo Buonarroti's "Pieta," 1500 – the marble sculpture completed when he was about 25 years old. It sits in the Basilica di San Pietro, Vatican City, Italy

INTRODUCTION:
A MANUAL FOR ARTISTS, WRITERS, AND OTHER CREATORS

The Master Artist Within was written for a good reason: It is the "secret manual for artists" that I wished I could find when I was a young artist. The quest for this material began when I was a teenager - a 16-year-old want-to-be-artist from a small town in the American South. All I wanted was to find the "meaning of life," and my home town school did not teach such things. To make things worse, the kind of art that I loved was not in fashion at that time. If I wanted to learn about the quality of art that was produced during the Renaissance, I had to study in Europe. The need for traveling money required selling my horse, my bicycle, and lying about my age to get a job. I then forged my mother's signature on a passport application and bought a ticket to cross the ocean. Like many young people at the time, I traveled with friends and stayed in youth hostels with other young backpackers. As fortune would have it, I ran out of money in Rome and had to find a job.

By some miracle, an Italian family hired me to take care of their children. Living with the family afforded me the ability to wander through every church and museum in Rome and obsess over a wealth of masterworks. Life on the small island where I grew up had not prepared me for what I experienced when faced with the overwhelming power of Italian Renaissance art, architecture, and sculpture. While studying the wealth of masterpieces, I felt both exhilarated and intimidated, inspired and overwhelmed, fortunate and unworthy.

One morning, I walked across Rome and entered St. Peter's Basilica at the Vatican. It was there that I had my first encounter with Michelangelo's *Pieta*. It took my breath away. That marble sculpture changed my life and my perception of reality. It wasn't so much the subject matter that stunned me, but a *mysterious energy* that radiated from the marble. It was the presence of the *artist who created it* that spoke to me.

At that time, the Pieta was relatively unprotected, so one could stand quite close – the viewer separated only by a red velvet rope. I could see every vein, muscle, hair, and fingernail. I could breathe in the magical air around the sculpture. Awestruck, I tried to imagine my humble self in the shoes of the artist. What was Michelangelo thinking? What force gave him an assumption that he could do such a thing? What power enabled him? A marble sculpture like this had never been done before, so where did he get the vision and determination to even begin? How did he know that it was even possible? These were the mysteries that I wanted to know about.

In my 16-year-old heart, a passionate prayer was formed on that spot – it was something like, "Whatever force that Michelangelo had flowing through him, that's all I want to know about." For my remaining months in Rome, I went once a week to stand in that same spot, trying to learn by osmosis how to be like Michelangelo.

After my time in Rome, life went on... I traveled, had many adventures, and became a young wife and mother. I created businesses, gardens, and homes, always looking for greater knowledge and a deeper meaning in everything. I studied interesting things, volunteered for projects, experimented with being an artist, baked lots of pies, tried to be the perfect mom, and had some pretty magnificent gardens. I learned a whole lot about ways to create in life - many positive, and many *not so positive*.

When my daughter eventually went away to college I was free to focus full-time on the kind of art that I had always loved. It was at this time that the forgotten prayer of my younger self, in the presence of Michelangelo's masterpiece, came flooding back to me... I had a revelation that sounded something like, "Oh God, why wasn't I living my life as my true self, and why was I not painting every day?" It felt like I had spent much of my life masquerading as much less than who I truly am. Simply creating was not enough. I wanted to experience what Michelangelo had experienced - the ability to create from my Soul. I decided to enroll in art classes to study painting, and in seminary classes to grow as a person.

I soon realized that the great mystery that I was looking for could not be found in any art school, instruction book, or academic theory. Art classes were not teaching how to get to the source of true Inspiration. Art books could not tell me how to create as my authentic self in the face of fear and self-doubt. Trying to find information about the origin of creative genius was like looking for the Holy Grail or the location of Atlantis. I combed the libraries of UCLA, the Getty Museum, the Smithsonian, European art centers, and esoteric bookstores. But no ancient manuscripts or "secret mystery school for artists" seemed to exist - and I really looked.

Painting full time to produce work for my doctoral degree, I was determined to paint as my "true self"- even though I had no idea *who* that was. While working in the studio, I faced a seemingly endless procession of creative fears, challenges, and inadequacies. I began to name and identify the artistic blocks that I had been avoiding my whole life.

I soon noticed that the inner spiritual work that I was doing did more to improve the quality of my painting than the art classes. It became evident that the time spent running, meditating, writing, and forgiving past experiences, was improving my work from the inside. My inner spiritual focus was having a dramatic effect on my creative ability and energy level. Very strange things began to happen. Curious about this phenomenon, I began to record and document what proved effective in overcoming the creative challenges, photographing the various stages of each painting. This turned out to be the beginning of what was to become *The Master Artist Within* methodology.

After years of work and experimentation, a simplified and user-friendly version of *The Master Artist Within* manual for artists has evolved. It is intended to be used by anyone creating anything, at any age, from any culture, or level of experience. I hope to offer encouragement to creative people experiencing periods of fear, doubt, or confusion. I wish you the very best in your own adventure to discover your innate creative genius, and the inner Master Artist in you.

HOW TO USE THE MASTER ARTIST WITHIN MANUAL

If you are an artist currently working with great enthusiasm at the top of your game, you may not want to invest your time reading this manual when you could be in the studio. *The Master Artist Within* is especially useful for those times when the creative person is experiencing some level of difficulty, or, they somehow *know* that their work could be better or more authentic, but don't know how to get there. During such times, this manual for artists can be a "road map" for how to get from where you are now, to where you want to go creatively - and maybe surprise yourself along the way.

Again, this is the "Secret Manual for Artists" that I *wished* I could find when I was a young artist. Throughout the book, we are reminded that "all art begins inside of the artist." These days, we have a world of good instruction for the different kinds of craft or skill required for every kind of art form. *The Master Artist Within* material is different. It is more for the *inner world* of the artist or creator wishing to find the *source* of their own genius, mastery, and Inspiration, regardless of the art form.

The human consciousness is a vast, complicated, and wondrous thing. No two are alike. Each one is a miracle. It is impossible to have one answer, one method, or one resolution that universally works for every artist's situation. I personally don't care for platitudes, convenient answers, or pre-formulated solutions for the creative issues that real people experience - so please forgive me if I ever give that impression.

The material in *The Master Artist Within* is based on personal, tried and true experience by real artists in a wide variety of situations. It is a treasure chest of tools and discoveries that any creative person can pick, choose, or experiment with on their journey from creative obstacle to creative freedom. As the transformation of a creative limitation often results in greater artistic ability, *The Master Artist Within* can be seen as a book of alchemy - empowering creative people to turn lead into gold.

Creative people can find themselves faced with obstacles and challenges that are sometimes difficult to define. We might experience anything from a simple lack of motivation, to something akin to a "dark night of the soul." *The Master Artist Within* is designed to address creative limitations - large or small - by transforming them in a way that encourages clarity, enthusiasm, authenticity, and surprising originality.

PART I answers the question: *who* and *what* is the Master Artist Within? It explains the nature of creative energy, and the many ways that we use it. The intention of reclaiming, and redirecting, our creative energy is introduced. We also investigate *who* or *what* it is inside of us that is making creative decisions.

PART II is the scary part - or the funny part, depending on your perspective. This is where we try to understand the nature of our creative blocks, limitations, and challenges *for the purpose of overcoming them*. Common creative difficulties that artists might face are organized into twelve "groups" for easier digestion. By identifying the obstacles that sabotage our work, we are better able to transform those obstacles into better art.

PART III introduces both the **Foundation Skills** and the **Tools for the Artist**. This is the transformational and empowering part. The Foundation Skills can be seen as lifestyle habits and techniques for supporting and encouraging creative people to do their best work. The Tools for the Artist are exercises for healing, clearing, and transformation. These games and exercises were specifically developed to transform the energy of any creative obstacle into the energy of creative mastery, genius, and authenticity.

I recommend first browsing through the whole manual to become familiar with what is available in *The Master Artist Within* material. Then you can pick, choose, or experiment with what you find most helpful in your current situation. Keep in mind that this book regards almost everything as a possible art form - from painting to gardening, from dance to city planning, from pottery to filmmaking. Once we learn how, we can apply the genius and enthusiasm of our inner Master Artist to just about any task at hand.

A WORD ABOUT METAPHOR AND MYTHOLOGY

Some experiences, especially *inner* experiences, are difficult to explain - especially for young art students. The beauty of using a metaphor is that we can use words, images, and archetypes to get down to the truth of something in a way that is more clear, more accessible, or easier to use.

I see much in the realm of language, images, and ideas in terms of metaphor. For example, I might use a word like "spirit" or "soul" to describe something that cannot be defined - referring to the *energy* in us that remains unaffected by our environment or experiences. Even creators who do not believe in a "higher power" know that creative genius does come from *somewhere* - so - it is that "somewhere" or "something" that we refer to when using lofty sounding words.

When I talk about the "Master Artist" in us, I am referring to a *state-of-being*, or a *zone*. This is the zone that we experience when we are happily and tirelessly creating *beyond* our usual or familiar ability. Many artists have mysteriously experienced amazing words, sounds, ideas, or pictures that just show up "out of thin air." We need a way to talk about such mysteries that are not explainable, so we invent words for the sake of communication. Metaphors give us a common language to understand each other. Like others, I know what it is to experience something so powerful that I become completely inarticulate and incapable of putting my experience into words or pictures. Thus, I assume that a great work of art that is truly Inspired has much more to it than what is apparent. If my words, explanations, or metaphors in *The Master Artist Within* offend you, please feel free to use terminology that works best for you. This material is intended as a helpful tool for artists and creators who wish to grow *beyond their current creative ability* - regardless of culture, situation, or language.

"I have had a vision. I have had a dream beyond the wit of man to say what dream it was. Man is but an ass if he go about t'expound this dream…"

William Shakespeare, *A Midsummer Night's Dream* 4:1

PART I

THE MYSTERY OF CREATIVE GENIUS, MASTERY, AND AUTHENTICITY

"Self Portrait" (at age 29) by German artist, painter and printmaker, Albrect Durer, 1500. Oil on wood panel 26.4" x 19.3" Alte Pinakothek, Museum in Munich, Germany.

1
WHO IS THE MASTER ARTIST WITHIN?

To be clear, the Master Artist Within is not a character waiting for the perfect moment to appear when no one is looking. Your inner Master Artist is a *state of being,* or a *zone*, that you experience when you create beyond your expected level of ability, often without knowing how or why. When our inner Master Artist produces something, we are usually very surprised by its quality. Wherever you are now in your artistic experience, you can learn how to allow your inner Master Artist to shine through your creative work more often.

Most people, whether they consider themselves artistic or not, have experienced creative mastery at some time in their life: The friend who unexpectedly says or does just the right thing at the right time. A loving mother who somehow makes a feast with inadequate resources. The neighbor on his back porch playing music that leaves you breathless... These can all be examples of spontaneous creative genius. Often, and without even trying, being in that innocent state of absolute love, truth, or enthusiasm opens a "magic door" to creative ability that is beyond our understanding. We can teach ourselves to open that "magic door" more often.

Our inner Master Artist is not predictable. It cannot be controlled or manipulated. It does not live in a particular place - it is always moving, growing, and learning. It is highly curious. For one to create with the originality of their inner Master Artist, one must be moving, growing, and learning to keep up with it. As artists cultivate a closer relationship with their inner Master Artist, their creative work will naturally become more original, authentic, and surprising.

As mysterious as it may sound, the ability to create with artistic mastery is available to everyone. How do we find our own inner Master Artist? It is often simply a matter of letting go of whatever stands in its way. Any student, artist, teacher, playwright, sculptor, engineer, performer, gardener, designer, or creator can experience their own inner Master Artist by redirecting how their creative energy is used. Whether you work alone, or on a team with other creative people, the world becomes a better place when we create from the best part of ourselves.

3 QUALITIES OF ARTISTIC MASTERY

I have found that there are three vital components to creating with Artistic Mastery: **Transcendence**, **Enthusiasm**, and **Authenticity**. Although these qualities can be called by other names, I find it helpful to keep these three words in mind as a way to check my attitude in the studio.

Transcendence: Transcendence is the willingness to reach beyond - beyond what we know, beyond what we have done before, beyond what we believe is possible, beyond our current awareness, and beyond what we believe we are capable of creating. Whether we call it growing, learning, listening, or exploring - when we open to transcending our past understanding, we are empowered to create with new abilities.

Enthusiasm: Enthusiasm can also be experienced as love, excitement, or Inspiration. It is an energizing and sustaining power. It provides the courage, motivation, vision, and willingness to begin a creative project - often completing it in a way that is beyond our imagining or expectation. The energy of true Enthusiasm often surpasses past experience because it has its own genius. Once we learn to work with Enthusiasm, we can bring that energy into even the most ordinary tasks.

Authenticity: Authenticity is the ability and willingness to express the truth of our True Self, or our Soul, when we are creating. Each artist is unique and has unique gifts. Whatever genius or Inspiration that we have inside of us, we can only access it through our True Self. The authentic expression of our soul, even though it can be awkward or inconvenient at times, is where we find the magic.

WHY ART?

What is art, and why are the arts so important? These questions have been asked many times. Art exists because humans have an innate need to express our inner truth, visions, or ideas in a way that cannot be fully expressed through other methods of expression or communication. We are not machines or objects. We are more than marketers or consumers. We are more than subjects to be used by forces outside of ourselves. Humans have a need to create and express who we truly are beyond mere skin and bones, beyond survival instincts, and beyond the world's conditioning. From ancient cave painting to the making of an epic movie, human beings have a need to travel beyond the known world through poetry, pictures, stories, movement, and new inventions.

We find that creators who have touched into the genius of Master Artist "energy" seem to transcend the laws of time and space, uplifting mankind with inspiration from "another place." When we see, hear, or read such timeless works of art, we are enraptured because they remind us of who we really are. The immortal quality in such works of art can "wake up" the part of us that is immortal, and help us to feel more alive, inspired, and hopeful.

Anything can be elevated to an art form. I have met plumbers, teachers, gardeners, speakers, healers, and computer wizards who become Master Artists in their own right, because the love and enthusiasm for their work transforms whatever they touch into a thing of beauty.

Artistry and *skill* are not the same thing. Skill can be learned from a book, teacher, or practice. Artistry must come from *within the creator* – the love of the artist breathes life into the skill. It is the inner artistic drive that will do what it must to acquire the skills it needs. Artistry will choose the best team for a creative project. Artistry keeps one working when the body is exhausted. Artistry creates beauty beyond what skill alone can achieve.

When most people speak of a Master Artist, they might refer to Mozart, da Vinci, Shakespeare, Sargent, O'Keefe, Chaplin, or others who are famous in various fields. But, as all humans are innately creative, there have been many Master Artists throughout history - many of them unknown or unacknowledged. For various reasons, some become more famous and are given more attention in history books - so, these artists wind up serving as archetypes when we talk about art. Although some ancient writers are known to us, it wasn't until relatively recent history that visual artists were given credit for their work. According to Renaissance historian Giorgio Vasari, Michelangelo chiseled his name across the marble heart of Mary in the middle of the night after hearing of another sculptor receiving credit for his masterpiece.

When reading the life stories of many Master Artists and innovators, it becomes clear that their creative mastery was not an accidental gift. Each one had their own obstacles and difficulties to transcend. Each one studied, practiced, and worked hard on their craft. Each one invested in the expansion and awakening of their "inner life." And, each one had an undying love for their work.

So... how do we get from where we are now, to *Master Artist* or *creative genius* territory? How do we get from a creative block to clarity, Inspiration, and enthusiasm? This is what The Master Artist Within manual is all about. The techniques in Part III can show you how to "redirect" your creative energy into greater mastery by *transforming* or *transcending* creative challenges. Understanding the Creative Obstacles in Part II is often enough for the artist to overcome them.

3 THINGS TO REMEMBER ABOUT MASTER ARTISTS

- Artistic mastery or genius is available to everyone, working in any art form, and at any level of experience.

- The *state of being* that produces original, masterful, and surprising works of art is achieved by transcending creative limitations.

- All masterpieces begin inside of the artist – you are your most valuable artistic tool.

Ultimately, creative genius happens as a result of some kind of transcendence, or *expansion* in the artist's consciousness. To transcend or expand in consciousness is to move *beyond* one's current experience, awareness, or perception into a higher perspective. Whether this "inner movement" happens because of learning something, transcending something, letting go of something, or experiencing something - our inner Master Artist can start creating something new when we least expect it.

The mind, with its limited understanding, cannot just "mock up" the Master Artist state of being. We can't pay anyone to produce it for us. Logic could not write the works of Shakespeare, business skill could not invent a Mozart aria, and opinions do not usually produce anything that is truly original. Such creations come through the unknown world of the human spirit - the domain of the Master Artist Within.

> "Inspiration is an awakening, a quickening of all man's faculties, and it is manifested in all high artistic achievements."
>
> Italian opera composer, Giacomo Puccini

CREATIVE AUTHENTICITY and THE TRUE SELF

"Authentic" is defined as "true, genuine, real...not fake or copied." All master works of art created throughout history were authentic and original to the artists who created them. For a creation to be original, it must be authentic. Authenticity means that we create work from our True Self - rather than some outside influence or conditioning, or the influence of our own fear, belief, or agenda. We could copy a Caravaggio painting to learn composition from a master, and *still be authentic* if our intent is to learn - rather than to steal, deceive, or plagiarize. We can all learn from Master Artists who went before us, and continue creating with our own authentic voice.

To grow into artistic mastery, why is it important for a creative person to strive for authenticity? Why should an artist investigate the nature of their True Self? It's all about the energy. Simply put, the *frequency* of truth, authenticity, and sincerity is empowering. Each artist has unique "inner gifts." If we withhold the magic and power of our inner gifts for the sake of "fitting in" or trying to be like someone else, we usually feel a sense of loss. As the artist becomes more confident in their authentic expression, they open the door for creative genius to appear.

Sometimes artists try to create like others to learn, practice, or experiment. We all learn from masters we admire. Growing into a more authentic voice is often just a matter of maturity. In certain cultures, people are not yet free enough to express their own true voice. It can take time to recognize the nature of our True Self and what it would create. Obviously, it can take great courage to be authentic in certain situations. The more we become familiar with the nature of our True Self, the easier it is to create with an authentic and original voice.

It can be pretty tricky to discern just *who* and *what* the True Self is. Playing the True Self/False Self Game in Part III is a very good way to explore and encourage greater authenticity, even if you're certain that you already know your True Self. There is always more to learn about your authentic voice. Becoming more familiar with your True Self will result in more authentic creative work without even thinking about it.

Creating in an authentic way does not mean that we have to rebel against everything in life. And, truth and authenticity is not an excuse to be unkind or disrespectful to others. Sometimes, of course, our authentic nature might move us to rebel when human rights are being violated. There is an art to discerning just how to use your creative energy at any given time. Qualities like cooperation, respect, and restraint are often just a matter of good manners, and important to world peace - both at home and on a global scale. Simple kindness is important for creating a better world. Master Artists can be good citizens, good neighbors, and good friends and still produce powerful, authentic, and original work.

When striving to create authentically, there is a phenomenon that I call the "Trail of Truth." I have found that if we *pay attention* to even the smallest and most insignificant of truths, that we are led to the next level of truth, and then the larger truth beyond that... All art begins with the artist. If we begin a painting or a story, and pay attention to what rings true to us in the moment, we may find unexpected revelations when the "Trail of Truth" creates a bridge into more authentic and original creations. Each artist is unique and has unique gifts. Creating authentically is the only way for that one-of-a-kind quality to show in our art.

3 THINGS TO REMEMBER ABOUT AUTHENTICITY

- All great works of art that have stood the test of time were true, authentic, and original to the artist who created them.

- Artists who cultivate their authentic voice can create unique art that no one else on earth is capable of creating.

- To be authentic and create original work, one must be loyal to the voice of their True Self, rather than current fashion, opinions, or other influences.

Astrophysicist Neil deGrasse Tyson says that we are created with atoms from the stars and have the whole universe inside of us. According to legend, Jesus said something like "These things you can also do, and even greater…" Leonardo da Vinci implied that we can actually become divine when we are painting. Are such ideas true? I am still investigating, but I tend to agree. We live in a complicated world where we have a daily opportunity to discover, and to create from, the best of who we are.

This Master Artist Within manual for artists was lovingly created for all humans wanting to create their best and most authentic work - as your Star Self, your Divine Self, your Greater Self - regardless of challenges.

> "His strength really lies in his imagination. A different imagination than some of us, but it's one you respect - And it's always slightly unexpected… on a rather larger scale…"

"David Lean: A life in Film," 1985

DIVINE INSPIRATION FOR HERETICS, PAGANS, AND MISFITS

In the following chapter, I use metaphors to describe an "Unknown World of creativity" - that magic place where we find qualities like Creative Genius, Originality, Mastery, Grace, or Divine Inspiration. It is the home of the artist's Muse, Angels, and Spirit Guides. Talking about the mystical aspects of creating can be tricky, because artists have many different cultures, faiths, and life experiences. So, for the sake of mutual respect and clear communication, I'll simply refer to this "mystical territory" by using one word most of the time. The qualities of this mythical Unknown World will simply be called *Inspiration*, with either a capital "I" or a small "i."

The simplest definition of the word *Inspiration* is basically what it sounds like - to inspire, or to breath in. It can also mean the mental or emotional stimulation to create or do something, or even a spiritual influence to receive other-worldly messages. For the inspiration that we feel after seeing a moving performance, the sudden desire to bake a cake, or the inspiration to go to the movies, we'll use *inspiration* with a small "i." For the more enduring type of *Inspiration* that sustains us with the sometimes superhuman vision, energy, and motivation to complete a new creative project, we will use a big "I."

True creative *Inspiration,* whether you think of it as *Divine* or not, seems to come from *beyond* our known experience, and *beyond* our current level of ability. It can't be explained because it comes from a place that is beyond what the mind can understand. This type of creative *Inspiration* is not limited to any particular religion or system of belief. Creating with *Inspiration* does, however, depend on our *willingness* to pay attention when we are fortunate enough to have the experience.

Is creative *Inspiration* a gift available to only a special group of people? Certainly not. All creative people can cultivate their inner Master Artist in a way that we can experience true creative *Inspiration* more often.

3 THINGS TO REMEMBER ABOUT INSPIRATION

- Creative Inspiration can happen to anyone and is not limited to any particular belief system or skill level.

- Creative Inspiration comes from *beyond* what the mind thinks, believes, or understands.

- Artists can cultivate their inner life in a way that invites creative Inspiration to happen more often.

ENCOURAGING MASTERY AND AUTHENTICITY IN YOUNG PEOPLE

Children and teenagers are often radiating with so much creative energy that adults don't know how to keep up with them. Often, when young people find themselves "in trouble," it is because they haven't learned how to use all that creativity in a better way. All children need love, support, guidance, and a good education to blossom into their best, bravest, and most authentic self.

It is vital for parents, teachers, coaches, and guardians to guide and encourage children to use their tremendous creative potential in the most healthy, uplifting, and positive way. Qualities like compassion, acceptance, and understanding others can be taught. It is important for leaders and lawmakers to understand that children are the future of the human race, and deserve to receive the respect, caring, protection, education, and encouragement that they need in order to share their gifts and inner genius with the world.

Teenagers in particular are powerful creators, and are therefore easily bored when not challenged with exciting, meaningful, and engaging work. Their creative energy is a powerful force that can be used in either positive or negative ways. Unguided creative energy can be channeled in ways that are either healthy or unhealthy, either helpful or harmful, either productive or destructive. History is full of young people who, with support and guidance, created and accomplished great things. With engaging education and encouragement, young people are capable of creating art, theater, literature, solutions, and inventions beyond our imagination.

If you are an art student or young creator, and have not received enough support, protection, and encouragement so far in your life - then start giving these things to yourself! There is always a way to find help if you need it. Adults are far from perfect. Many have gone through difficult experiences. And some lack the ability to see clearly. Forgive them - and be determined to use your creative gifts to create with your own unique kind of artistic mastery and authenticity. Guidance counselors, older artists, and master creators in their field often enjoy advising and guiding sincere young artists. With a bit of research, one can find grants, scholarships, and organizations dedicated to promoting the arts. Above all, take excellent care of yourself and those close to you. Work hard on your art form. Be kind, honest, and cultivate friendships with good people. Always create at the best of your ability, in any situation, with what you have to work with, and Artistic Mastery will continue to grow in you.

NOTES

"Astronomer by Candlelight" (detail), 1650's, by Dutch painter, Gerrit Dou. Oil on wood panel, 12 5/8 x 8 3/8, Getty Museum, Los Angeles, California.

2

THE "TWO WORLDS" OF CREATIVITY

First of all, what exactly is creativity? Creativity is an energy, a motivating force, that urges us to do, make, or express something. All humans have it. For artists and creative people, creativity begins with a spark, an idea, or vision that is translated through our skill, our energy, and our current state of being. Like a wind, or an electric current, creativity can also motivate us to make changes, or even to tear something down. Creative energy can also encourage us to research, explore, or learn something new. It's the energy of love, life, Inspiration, change, and evolution.

A creative impulse is so powerful because it tends to involve every aspect of the artist. When our thoughts, our feelings, our spirit, and our physical energy are all unified and excited about the same creative vision at the same time, wonderful things can happen. Masterpieces are painted, babies are born, and symphonies are written. On the other hand, if our mind has one agenda, but our heart wants to create something else, our body just wants to look at food, and our spirit self isn't interested in any of it…. Well, that is the recipe for a big fat creative block. As creative people, it becomes important to know ourselves well, to take excellent care of our well-being, and to use our creative energy in ways that are both positive and challenging.

Every human who has ever lived has had the experience of creating things. When someone tells me something like, "I don't have a creative bone in my body," I have to laugh. We can't get through our day without making creative decisions. From mud huts to palaces, from arrowheads to airplanes, from blueberry pies to computers - we are undeniably creative beings. We help create the world with every decision we make. With every interaction with another, with every purchase we make, with every thought we entertain, and especially with the things that we teach our children, we become powerful creators of the world we live in. That can be a scary responsibility to consider. The important thing is to decide what we, as artists and creators, want to create with the relatively brief amount of time that we have here on this planet.

There is no shortage of creative energy, although it may feel that way at times. Just like our lungs are always breathing and our heart is always beating, creative energy is always flowing through us. Even deciding what to make for breakfast is a creative decision. In fact, our creative energy can get us into big trouble if not channeled wisely. Just like simple water can take the form of snow, steam, or clouds, our creative energy can take many forms. If, for example, one has channeled a lot of creative energy into making a mess in life, that same creative energy can be *redirected* into producing wonderful things. It all depends on our awareness and *who* inside of us is *directing* our valuable creative energy.

There are so many reasons why we create the way we do, and why we experience challenges at times. Creative energy that is influenced by strong emotional feelings might become a beautiful opera or a lot of unnecessary drama. Creative energy, influenced by a belief system, might create a homeless shelter or a hate crime. Creative energy that is directed by a brilliant mind might find a cure for disease or plan a bank robbery. Our education might empower us to create beautiful works of art, or, cause us to create according to someone else's ideas. And when our creative energy is scattered by differing opinions and motivations, we might create all kinds of diversions to just avoid the inner chaos.

Master Artists are creators who have found a way to recognize, follow, and listen to the authentic voice of their True Self. In the Master Artist Within methodology, we refer to two different sources of creativity: The **Known World**, and the **Unknown World**. Of course, these "Two Worlds" of creativity are just metaphors for talking about different sources of motivation that are difficult to define.

The Known World: The first of these "Two Worlds" of creativity is our familiar *Known World*. In this *Known World*, we get ideas, images, and motivation from all of our education, history, beliefs, media, pictures, assumptions, experiences, and everything in the universe that has "already been created." It represents the status quo. We have thousands of years' worth of ideas and materials to draw upon, and there is a lot to influence how we think and what we create. Creatively, we can even consider unconscious impulses as part of our *Known World* because our unconscious or subconscious parts can act as "storage space" for known experiences, even if we don't remember them. The old cliché that cites, "There is nothing new under the sun," exists because most of what is created every day is really a "restructuring" of ideas and things from the vast already-created *Known World*. It is hard to create anything truly original when relying on the *Known World* as your *only* source of inspiration.

Creating in the *Known World* can be safe and predictable. It can also be the source of fear, beliefs, prejudices, and things to avoid. There are established rules in the *Known World*. We might justify anything that we create, or don't create, according to a precedent of something that has happened in the *Known World*. This can be useful when trying to duplicate a favorite recipe or drive a car safely - but not so useful when a *Known World* precedent becomes a creative limitation. We have many wonderful things in our *Known World*, but it obviously has its limitations. Miraculous things have been created by artists who have dared to go beyond the safety of the *Known World*. As Shakespeare's Hamlet told his friend, "There are more things in Heaven and Earth, Horatio, than are dreamt of in your philosophy…"

The Unknown World: The second source of creativity is the *Unknown World*, which is the domain of all that has not yet come into being. This *Unknown World* is the source of anything truly original. Creative geniuses who have given us works of art that have long stood the "test of time" had the ability to access their inner Unknown World. Although some may call such creativity *genius* or *Divine Inspiration*, this is not a superhuman feat available only to a special few. Without realizing it, ordinary people regularly tap into this *Unknown World* when they "accidentally" say something brilliant, or come up with a completely original design, or solve a problem beyond their usual level of ability.

We have so many examples of *Inspired* and original works of art, music, architecture, theater, and other creations that originated in the mysterious *Unknown World*. Oddly, such works seem to defy the laws of time and space by retaining their beauty and value to mankind, regardless of their age or culture. Masterful creations are important to mankind because they remind us that being human can be a dignified, mysterious, and beautiful thing. In a world where new things can become old news very quickly, Inspired works often become more beautiful, powerful, and uplifting as time passes.

The artist's ability to bring original ideas and visions from the *Unknown World* into our *Known World* makes them a powerful force in the universe. One reason that a computer could never fully replace a human artist is this: Computers must depend on entered data and programming from the already-created *Known World*. But human beings have the ability to transcend the *Known World* and travel into their spirit to gather new ideas, visions, and *Inspiration* from the not-yet-created *Unknown World*. Just as in Shakespeare's use of the English language or Michelangelo's use of raw marble, elements from the *Known World* can transmute and become alive in the hands of a Master Artist.

Transcendence produces energy. When we learn to transcend our creative difficulties and limitations, the *movement* of that transcendent energy gives us greater access to the *Inspiration* and creativity of the *Unknown World*. Truly original and *Inspired* works of art can't be faked or imitated because they vibrate with a unique frequency. Using our inner "radio tuner" as a metaphor, the Master Artist "zone" resonates with a different frequency on our dial than other sources of creativity. The Foundation Skills and Tools for the Artist in Part III are designed to help artists, students, and creative people to "tune in" to their inner Master Artist, regardless of the challenges along the way.

3 THINGS TO REMEMBER ABOUT CREATIVITY

- As all humans are powerful creators, it is important to be aware of how we are using our creative energy - both inwardly and outwardly.

- To create with genius, mastery, and originality, the artist goes *beyond* what they have thought or experienced before.

- When we learn to transcend our creative difficulties and limitations, the *movement* of that transcendent energy gives us greater access to the *Inspiration* and creativity of the *Unknown World*.

"I shall give to you what no ear has heard and what no man has touched and what has never occurred to the human mind."

Thomas 17, from the *Nag Hammadi Library*

"Joan of Arc As Shepherdess" (detail) 1889, by Jules Eugene Lenepveu.
The first of four mural panels in the Pantheon, Paris, France.

3

RECLAIMING AND REDIRECTING YOUR CREATIVE ENERGY

What does it mean to "reclaim" or "redirect" one's creative energy? Occasionally, our creative energy can be used in the creation of things or actions that we never really wanted in the first place. Or, our energy might be scattered between so many projects that our most important work winds up being compromised. As we become more aware of *how* our valuable creative energy is being used, we can *reclaim* any unused or misdirected energy - and *redirect* it into better work.

All art begins with the artist. So, when the artist's creative energy is being influenced by a fear, a limiting belief, an overriding agenda, or other complications, much of their creative energy can be trapped or misdirected. The creative person's focus and energy might be used, scattered, or diverted into creating far below what they are actually capable of creating. It's hard for any artist to create with mastery and authenticity with issues draining their creative power. But, once we learn to recognize when, how, or why this is happening, it becomes easier for our inner Master Artist to direct how our creative energy is being used.

We'll call anything that *interferes* with an artist's ability to create their best and most authentic work a "Creative Obstacle." Anything that *negatively influences* how a creative person works is also a Creative Obstacle. Once the artist is able to inwardly transform or overcome their Creative Obstacle, they can *reclaim* the creative energy what was once trapped or misdirected. The creative person is then free to *redirect* their creative focus, energy, and enthusiasm into creating work that they love, often with new levels of artistic ability.

Creative Obstacles are made of energy - energy that takes the form of blocks, fears, limitations, confusion, or other types of creative challenges. As we learn to inwardly transform our Creative Obstacles, we can *reclaim* and *redirect* how that energy is being used. **Part II** of this manual is all about identifying possible Creative Obstacles for the purpose of transforming them. The *Foundation Skills* and the *Tools for the Artist* in **Part III** provide ways to *reclaim and redirect* your creative energy into greater joy, clarity, mastery, and originality.

Where do our creative blocks, fears, limitations, or other challenges come from? How do these Creative Obstacles even get into our inner world in the first place? Who and what directs our creativity into creating the things that we do not even want? The possibilities are many: Our life experiences. Our culture or religion. Our creative fears. Self-judgments. Childhood experiences. Media programming. Social conditioning. Limiting beliefs. Current fashion. Survival instincts. Mean people. Feelings of lack or inadequacy. Our education or lack thereof. The rules of life that we either have or have not agreed to. Not to mention the many psychic influences of which we are not even consciously aware. Regardless of the cause, we can transform any creative challenge into better work.

It is important to remember that creative work, for better or worse, always originates in the inner world of the artist. Both Creative Obstacles *and* Creative Genius live within the creative person's "inner world." Thus, the transformation of Creative Obstacles into Creative Genius happens within our inner world. The *redirection* of creative energy must happen in *your* inner world before it can physically manifest in your art. Friends have called this called this dynamic the "quantum physics of creativity." According to the laws of thermodynamics, energy is never destroyed. It only changes form. We can change the form of our energy and begin to create with more love, mastery, enthusiasm, and originality.

THE ILLUSION OF BUSY WORK

Some artists find that they have a tremendous amount of creative energy tied up in what we'll call "busy work." Perhaps the simplest illustration of *busy work* is a dog chasing his tail. Instead of running across a field or chasing ducks, he chases his own tail round and around in circles - pretending that he's doing something vitally important when nothing is really going on. The dog becomes exhausted, using a lot of energy on an illusion. If the dog could become aware of his actions, he might break free and start chasing real ducks.

Busy work might look like spending too much time cleaning, researching, organizing, or running errands. It often takes the form of doing so many things for other people that there is no time to grow creatively. Some artists create so much chaos or disagreement that they are constantly running around "putting out fires" or "solving problems." Creating predictable art that is far below our true ability can also be just another form of busy work. Our actions become busy work when we go out of our way to create unnecessary ways to avoid the studio, and the creative challenges that may be waiting for us there. Once we realize what we're doing, we can redirect our creative energy into the creations that are most important to us.

When an artist has created a lot of *busy work*, the reasons are often based on some kind of resistance, avoidance, or fear. Whether there is a fear of failure, a fear of success, a fear of discovering a greater self, a fear of losing something, or a fear of the unknown - as long as we are *busy*, we don't have time to face those fears.

Creating work of a quality that is beyond our comfort zone, and beyond our current experience level, requires that we *do something different*. Busy work might seem easier than facing the fear, inadequacy, or other dragons standing between us and our next level of creative ability, but it is not our friend. Once we become aware of such avoidance, our valuable creative energy can be *reclaimed* and *redirected* into work that allows our inner genius, enthusiasm, and artistic mastery to shine through.

Not all of our daily actions outside of the studio are busy work... The time that we spend taking care of ourselves, our environment, and our loved ones can actually *strengthen* our creative mastery. Anything done in love or compassion can be a creative act. Experiences that strengthen our inner character, happiness, and sense of humor can also strengthen our creative work. Only the individual artist can decide what is time-wasting busy work - and what is important for a happy and healthy life. When unsure, I often ask myself questions like, "Will this make a difference in the quality of my life or work? ...in a month from now? ...in a year? ...in a generation?"

The first step in *reclaiming* your creative energy is being honest with yourself about *what and how you really want to create*. Sometimes this is known to the artist, and sometimes it takes a bit of soul-searching. The thing that we most want to create can be as simple as friendship, or as big as an international organization. There may be times when our greatest artistic desire is simply to learn or explore. Once an artist envisions a project that is vibrating with Inspiration, excitement, and enthusiasm, they become more willing to fight for it. It can be hard to make serious life changes for something that doesn't really matter in your heart of hearts. Whether your motivation is to create is a film, a family, a novel, a series of paintings, a new invention, or even a new community - it is important to be absolutely honest with yourself, regardless of how simple or impossible the vision or Inspiration may seem at the time.

3 THINGS TO REMEMBER ABOUT CREATIVE ENERGY

- We can reclaim our creative energy that is trapped in the form of fear, doubt, agendas, overwhelm, resistance, or false beliefs.

- Our creative energy is always creating *something*, and it is the artist's job to direct it in a positive way with truth, mastery, and authenticity.

- When energy takes the form of a creative block, that energy can be transformed into clarity, enthusiasm, and new levels of artistic ability.

Keep in mind that what the *personality* wants, what the *False Self* wants, or what we have been *conditioned* to want, may not be the same thing that our inner Master Artist is Inspired to create. Once the artist becomes clear about what they want to create - even if it's only in part - it is important to record it in your Private Journal. Some people call this act of writing down your creative vision an *intention*, *a dream*, or *setting a goal*. For some people (like me) pictures and drawings often work better than words. This act of recording your creative visions is important for this reason: When life gets busy, we can become sidetracked or bogged down with busy work and lose sight of what is most vital to our inner artist. Creating your own Guiding Star (page 169) will help you to stay on track with what is most important. In a busy and complicated world, it takes vigilance to keep one's creative energy directed in a true, masterful, uplifting, and authentic way.

Another important way to keep our creative energy directed according to our inner Master Artist is though movement. There is something about physical exercise that supports mental clarity, a sense of well-being, and our ability to stay focused. Movement, sweating, stretching, and deep breathing all help to release sluggish or disturbing energies. Walking and running work. Dancing works. Gardening works. Hiking works. Yoga works. Find out what best encourages mental clarity, inner awareness, and a sense of well-being for the artist in you.

According to some philosophies, creativity corresponds with the body's chakra called Svadhisthana - located in the region of the body between the knees and navel. This makes sense, as this is where procreation happens and where babies grow - the most amazing of all creations. Many creative people find that this region of body is sensitive and may require extra protection. When we *withhold* our creative energy, it can "back up" and cause problems in this part of the body - creating such conditions as constipation, infections, and weight gain. This is another reason to keep our creative energy flowing in a positive way. Physical movement, and exercises like yoga or dance can clear out stuck energies and enliven our creative energy. Learning to master how we *use* and *direct* our creative energy, and how to make ourselves available to our inner source of genius and Inspiration, is what becoming a Master Artist is all about.

"There is no exercise to restore "the creative," only the secret of turning the light around. The light itself is the creative; to turn it around is to restore it."

From *The Secret Of the Golden Flower: The Classical Chinese Book of Life,* translated by Thomas Cleary

NOTES

"Rain and Bullet" (detail) 1986, watercolor on paper 28 x 22. An early example of trying to teach myself how to paint people.

4

FIRST, CREATE YOUR SECRET JOURNAL OR SKETCHBOOK

When working toward creative mastery, it is important to have a Secret Journal. A "top secret" sketchbook, notebook, or journal becomes a valuable tool for the artist for this reason: As we go into new and unknown territory, we need a private *holding place* for our discoveries, questions, and revelations. During the Master Artist Within journey, the artist's Secret Journal can become a friend in times of trouble, and a treasure chest of original ideas to draw upon when feeling distracted.

Like the dreams that we have while sleeping, new visions and new revelations can be fleeting. When we receive images, sounds, ideas, or Inspiration from the unconditioned energy of the Unknown World, they can be as fragile as the morning dew that evaporates with the rising sun. We need a place to write down, record, or sketch such gifts before they evaporate from our awareness. It becomes important to support the growth of the inner artist by documenting his or her own unique creative "vision quest."

There is a long tradition of Master Artists, scientists, and philosophers who kept journals to record ideas, sketches, revelations, and experiments. Private writing can be a powerful tool for uncovering hidden aspects of the creator's inner world, protected from the eyes and opinions of those not on your journey. This can be anything from a spiral notebook to a fancy artist's sketchbook - as long as it is both durable and portable. Anything too fancy or expensive might interfere with the freedom to make a mess - and to grow as artists, we need the freedom to make a mess, to explore, and to change our mind as we evolve.

It is better to have a traditional paper journal or sketchbook, rather that writing with a computer or other machine. This is because there is something magical that comes through the human hand - in writing, drawing, and in working things out. The human hand has a wisdom that a keyboard just does not have. Also, we need to have access to our journal at inconvenient or strange times, and computers are not always available. (As those of us living in hurricane territory know) Lie detector tests work because our bodies have a connection to the truth that may be hidden from us. When we write, mold, or draw something with our hands, something of our spirit is transported through the action. There are times when the human touch can be more healing than medicine because it is capable of transmitting love, light, healing, and the soul's intelligence. In much the same way, writing and drawing in our journal by hand can open the door to more of our wisdom, truth, and Inspiration.

The object of all of the exercises and lessons in *The Master Artist Within* material is to go *beyond* what we already know, or what we already *think* we know. Often, in going *beyond* our current creative ability, and *beyond* our current way of seeing things, we are very surprised by what we find. The artist's Secret Journal becomes the witness and the proof of our successes, discoveries, and what we have learned when the voices of doubt come back around to haunt us (as they often do).

The artist's Secret Journal, or Sketchbook, can also be a receptacle for pictures, music, dreams, or information that is somehow important to the artist's journey, even if it does not make sense at the time. An artist might, for example, see a picture of a gorilla in a magazine that gives them a spark of inspiration. There may be no explanation for why this image of a gorilla has so grabbed their attention, but they know that it is something important. Chances are, there is something about that image, a clue to some inner mystery, that is not yet clear to the artist. The picture can be taped into the journal - either to lose its importance in time, or perhaps becoming part of some future work. Often, things that we are drawn to - sights, sounds, shapes, words, colors, etc., turn out to represent something important inside of us that we cannot yet identify. We can make a note about a piece of music that really moves us, a line in a film that gave us goosebumps, or a new art material to try. Like a scout following the "Trail of Truth," we pay attention to the hidden clues that lead us toward the enthusiasm of our inner Master Artist.

An important part of learning how to create with more mastery, enthusiasm, originality, and authenticity is the artist's growing discovery of their True Self. The artist's Secret Journal becomes a vital tool in a creative person's ability to sort out the difference between the creative instincts of the True Self, and other sources of motivation. Only the True Self holds the keys to authenticity. A life of conditioning, limiting beliefs, and preconceived notions can all compete to take control of our creative energy - producing inauthentic and unoriginal work according to their limitations. The more comfortable and familiar that we become with our True Self, the more we are able to master how our creative energy is being used. The Secret Journal is used for the True Self/False Self Game in Part III - a valuable exercise for discovering more about one's True Self.

It usually doesn't work to sit down and think, "OK, now I'm going to write or draw something really profound in my Secret Journal." We begin by simply sketching or telling ourselves the truth as it is right now, regardless of how mundane, silly, or seemingly inconsequential. This works for the artist because a tiny little truth leads us down the path the to the next truth, and then the next, and then the even bigger truth after that. In our Secret Journal, we collect pictures that we love. We sketch images from a mysterious dream. We experiment with colors. We record formulas for glazes. We write down sudden flashes of insight before we lose them. We might tear out passages that turned out to be only temporarily true for us. The Secret Journal is ours, and we don't need to explain it to anyone.

So why is it so important for the artist's Secret Journal to be regarded as "top secret?" The *intention* of the Master Artist Within material is to encourage greater mastery, greater originality, and greater authenticity - so it helps to feel free from the opinions and judgments of others. We need to protect ourselves from the temptation to impress others at the cost of being less real with ourselves. We might have absolute respect from and for the people around us. We might be confident that they would never judge us. We may even tell ourselves that we don't care what others think. Still, some part of us *does* care, and might edit, embellish, or hold back certain discoveries if we feel that another's eyes might see it.

Once we are 100% confident that we are the only ones to see what we record or put into our Secret Journal, we are freer to explore, to be different, to sound crazy, to be grandiose, or even to make no sense at all. Often, what we find on the trail between where we are, and where we are going, can be so foreign to our current life that we may not be comfortable with how we really feel. (A big, tough, motorcycle enthusiast may need the creative freedom to draw pictures of kittens or bunnies in their Secret Journal without having to justify or explain it to anyone.) In centuries past, people have been ridiculed or persecuted for daring to look beyond the accepted status quo. We might even have unconscious, built-in fears about "being different" that make no sense to us at all - so the more freedom that we give ourselves to express what the inner artist is exploring, the safer we feel to go into unknown creative territory. So, out of respect for your inner Master Artist, try to keep your Secret Journal as confidential as possible.

3 THINGS TO REMEMBER ABOUT KEEPING A SECRET JOURNAL OR SKETCHBOOK

- Artists need a place to record discoveries about their own inner creative journey that is free form the opinions of others, or the temptation to impress others.

- Recording the truth about what we love, what we dream, and what awakens our enthusiasm can lead to even greater inner truth.

- It is important to manually write and draw because the human hand has a wisdom that a keyboard just does not have.

"My work has escaped from my control, and I have produced a monster…" Written by English author, JRR Tolkien, in a 1950 letter to Sir Stanley Unwin while working on the *Lord of the Rings Trilogy. The Letters of J.R.R. Tolkien,* edited by Humphrey Carpenter and Christopher Tolkien

PART II

CREATIVE OBSTACLES: UNDERSTANDING ARTISTIC BLOCKS, LIMITATIONS, AND CHALLENGES

"The First Maine Fishermen" (detail) 1937 by N.C. Wyeth, used as an illustration for *Trending Into Maine* by Kenneth Roberts. Oil on hardboard panel, about 35 x 25, private collection.

5

RECOGNIZING CREATIVE OBSTACLES

The Master Artist Within manual defines a "Creative Obstacle" as anything that *interferes with*, or *negatively influences*, an artist's ability to do their best creative work. A Creative Obstacle might look like a block, a fear, confusion, an agenda, a limiting belief, or other type of challenge that the artist is experiencing when trying to work.

Each artist and creative person is unique and inventive. They can experience an infinite variety of Creative Obstacles that range from a simple lack of instruction, to a paralyzing fear. Some Creative Obstacles can seem complicated, entangled, or tricky. So, for the sake of greater clarity and understanding, PART II is organized into 12 "groups" of Creative Obstacles. Gaining awareness about the many possible creative fears, blocks, and other challenges can be used to *untangle* their effect, freeing the artist of their influence. Often, simply *understanding* how a Creative Obstacle works is enough to transform its energy into better and more authentic work. Recognizing or acknowledging a creative challenge can be the first step in overcoming it.

Some Creative Obstacles have things to teach us before they can be transformed into our next level of artistic ability. The important thing is that we do not judge or dwell on our challenges, but simply bring our awareness to them long enough to transcend them. Occasionally, our obstacles can be quite good at disguising how they undermine our creative work. Whether the Creative Obstacle is a limiting belief, a hidden agenda, a type of fear, or a collection of competing motivations - any obstacle can be *transformed* into greater creative ability.

Overcoming a Creative Obstacle can begin with an artist being honest with themselves about what they truly want to create. As creative people, we can be so inventive when it comes to avoiding, denying, or overcompensating for imagined limitations that we can lose track of our biggest creative dreams. For example, if a feeling of "unworthiness" is the dragon that stands between an artist and how they want to create, that artist might rather walk across a desert than face the feared dragon. The Tools for the Artist in Part III will provide all kinds of help for turning such dragons into friends and allies - when the artist is ready and willing.

The truth about Creative Obstacles is this: Artists, writers, researchers, inventors, scientists, and all creators have always been on the *frontier*, or the *cutting edge* of bringing new creations into the world. Being on that forefront, creative people naturally run into challenges that stand between where they are now, and the next level of creator that they are becoming. If you are currently facing big creative challenges, it may be a good sign. You just may be a creator in a "growth stage," where unimaginable things are possible.

How can we tell if we are dealing with a Creative Obstacle? If you look at your work, or especially a *lack* of work, and wish for something better - then there is probably something standing in your way. It's important to remember the good news: Every creative block, challenge, or limitation is a golden opportunity to become a better artist. Paradoxically, the transformation of a Creative Obstacle can result in a greater artistic ability than if one had never experienced the obstacle in the first place.

Once we start to observe or understand a Creative Obstacle, it starts to lose the power that it has over us. There is a magic to where we place our attention or focus. As in quantum physics, bringing our *awareness* to something has its own transformative power and influence. Observing or naming a creative challenge is important for this reason: A Creative Obstacle *depends* upon our tendency to avoid, ignore, tolerate, make excuses, or deny their existence.

Our inner Master Artist is often Inspired to create work that is beyond our "comfort zone." The fear of discovering a "greater self" can be very real. The fear of persecution for surpassing others can be very real. Sometimes, we hold onto our creative limitations because they feel safe, familiar, and predictable. In order to protect us from imagined harm, a

Creative Obstacle might argue for its right to exist. Therefore, it may take courage to let go of, or to transcend, our creative limitations in order to experience what our inner genius or Master Artist might create.

A **creative limitation** could be easily transformed if it's just a need for more education, experience, or awareness. These days, the internet holds a wealth of information and instruction - some of it actually quite good. A creative limitation might simply be a result of where the artist is working, or the people in the environment. It could be a need for more exercise or better nutrition to increase circulation and feed the brain cells. A limitation might be misinformation, superstition, or a limiting belief that the artist has adopted along the way. There are times when the rules and beliefs about your art form should be challenged to see whether they are true or not. Usually it takes the artist's willingness, and determination, to make sure that they have the instruction, environment, supplies, and care they need to do their best creative work.

A **creative challenge** usually requires the artist to grow *beyond* how they currently create. Trying to stay the same, or stay comfortable, or hold onto what is familiar can interfere with an artist's ability to create with the quality or originality that is desired. The challenge could be an inner conflict, an agenda pressing on the mind, a lack of motivation, or any number of issues. A challenge could be too much concern about the opinion of other people. A creative challenge often robs the artist of the joy and enthusiasm of creating, resulting in work that is less inspired or original than it possibly could be. The artist can reclaim a lot of creative power by overcoming things that challenge their creativity.

A **creative block** is perhaps the most sabotaging of the Creative Obstacles. When an artist is suffering with a creative block, they may find it difficult to work at all. Often, a creative block is a result of misused, misdirected, or withheld creative energy because of some underlying fear. Sometimes the artist doesn't feel capable of what they most want to do or say in their work, or, the artist has too many conflicting inner directions to get started on any one thing. Our valuable creative energy, when withheld, can take the form of drama, weight gain, depression, addictions, negative thinking, or any number of sabotaging situations. Blocks usually appear before crossing the bridge into the next level of artistic ability. When an artist overcomes or transforms a creative block, it usually results in surprising work that goes beyond what they once imagined.

FEAR, PAIN, CONFUSION, AND OTHER DRAGONS: TWELVE TYPES OF CREATIVE OBSTACLES

The following 12 Chapters describe a variety of possible Creative Obstacles. These common Creative Obstacles are similar at times. They are related in strange ways, and often influence and reinforce each other. The organization of the next 12 Chapters is intended to help the artist, student, or creative team to identify what they need to know in order to transform or transcend their creative issues.

Having the willingness and courage to look at the true nature of a creative block, limitation, or challenge, is the first step in overcoming it. Often, artists spend so much time denying, hiding, or overcompensating for a creative limitation that the very thought of actually facing it head-on can be a bit scary. I have been there many times.

The good news is that once we *identify, observe,* or *understand* a creative challenge, we can begin to transform its energy into better art. When these transformations happen, there is a mysterious and undeniable alchemy at work. New energy, enthusiasm, and artistic ability usually result after transcending or transforming a Creative Obstacle.

So, how do we *begin* this process of transforming our Creative Obstacles? Step one is to take an honest look at what we would truly want to create if anything were possible, and then write down the reasons for not doing it. Some artists, assuming that there is nothing that can be done about a creative difficulty, find it difficult to even acknowledge their biggest dreams or the obstacles standing in their way. Even though it may be hard to believe at times, creative people are bigger and more powerful than their current circumstances.

Some of the material in this section may be difficult to read at times. Reading about Creative Obstacles can make an artist angry, rebellious, defensive, offended, embarrassed, and declare that it is all horse manure. Sometimes we hold so fiercely onto our creative limitations because they represent the security of familiar ground. Creative limitations are predictable, comfortable, and protect us from the risks associated with becoming an unknown and more powerful creator. So, we might fight for our right to keep our creative limitations - until the inner Master Artist says that "enough is enough," and decides that it's time to shine.

THE EMPOWERMENT OF OWNING YOUR CREATIVE OBSTACLES

There is an important thing to consider when reading about the following types of Creative Obstacles: It helps to "own everything." By *owning everything*, I mean that regardless of *where* a creative block or limitation came from, or *how* it originated, or *who* is to blame for it, we can claim *ownership* over it. If we pin the ownership of our creative difficulties on someone else through blaming, we then give them "power" over us and our creativity. Regardless of who or what caused a creative limitation, the artist is *most empowered* to transform the limitation once they completely *own* the situation. The energy contained in our creative difficulties is *our* energy. If the Creative Obstacle remains the "fault" of something or someone else - even our own genetics - then to some degree, it becomes more difficult to transform it. As challenging as this may be at times (for some have experienced horrendous things), *owning* the creative difficulty at hand gives you the right and authority to reclaim and redirect how you use your own creative energy. Even if this sounds crazy, I encourage you to experiment with this idea when using the tools in Part III.

TRANSFORMING A CREATIVE CHALLENGE

Metaphorically, we can look at everything that an artist produces as a form of energy. Even our messes and mistakes are composed of our energy. An artist's creative energy can take the form of a normal day of work, or something truly original and magnificent. It all depends on our *state of being,* *how we use* our creative energy, and *who inside of us* is making each creative decision. Simply put, energy that does take the form of a creative challenge can be *transformed, reclaimed, and redirected* into more original and masterful works of art. The art of transforming an artistic challenge into artistic mastery can be kind of like turning compost into flowers or garbage into fuel.

With a little imagination (and a sense of humor) the examples in the next 12 chapters are probably enough help you to define *your own* unique challenges and begin the process of transforming them. You might add some of your own descriptions to the list. You may find that the different Creative Obstacles can all be interconnected at times - influencing each other in a "matrix" that can take patience to untangle. They may seem to shape-shift and change at times. Remember that the only reason to identify them at all is to transform their energy into better creative work and happier artists. The **Tools for the Artist** exercises in Part III were created specifically to transform even the trickiest of creative challenges, empowering artists to reclaim their creative energy - if the artist is ready and willing.

DRAGON MYTHOLOGY

Often, I choose to look at different kinds of creative difficulties as imaginary "Dragons." This began years ago in my Santa Barbara studio while working on a series of paintings that required a far greater level of artistic ability than I had. Being faced with a seemingly insurmountable Creative Obstacle, I started writing in order to get to the bottom of the fear and inadequacy that I was experiencing. After some time into the writing exercise, something like a mini "opera" started pouring out of me and onto the yellow legal pad that I was using. Having no musical talent and knowing nothing about composition, this was quite a shock - but I kept writing. In the emerging story, one Dragon after another presented itself, along with instructions on how to tame each one. Some unknown part of me, with a bizarre sense of humor, was giving me a lesson in transforming my creative limitations into a new level of artistic vision and ability.

Seeing a creative challenge as a "Dragon," or some other imaginary creature, can help the artist or student to see limitations in a more humorous and objective way. For the purpose of reclaiming our creative energy, these Dragons are not to be fought or killed, as they represent a *part of us* and hold valuable creative energy. The more creative and empowering choice is to tame, embrace, and re-educate our Dragons to better serve our inner Master Artist. At the end of a tough day in the studio, I've often joked with friends about my day of "dragon taming."

In Waldorf schools, children perform a beautiful Michelmas play each fall that involves a colorful Dragon and a whole cast of characters. The purpose of the Michelmas Play is to demonstrate to the students how to *tame* the Dragon, and "make it work for light and love again" - preparing the children for the school year with a bold heart and self-confidence. In much the same way, we can teach our own creative Dragons to work for light, love, and our inner Master Artist.

I include an example of my own Dragons with each of the following Creative Obstacles, together with what I might do to tame each one. If you find this exercise useful, you can experiment with describing and taming your own Creative Dragons - recording in your Secret Journal what you learn about their transformation. Remember that the whole point is to reclaim and redirect your valuable creative energy, and to bring love and light into any fearful parts of your inner world.

USING THE CREATIVE OBSTACLE CHECKLISTS

While reading about the Creative Obstacles described in Part II, remember this: The whole reason and purpose for trying to *identify* Creative Obstacles, as they occur, *is to be able to transform them into greater artistic ability*. Each of the following 12 Chapters also has a "Checklist" of words or phrases to consider, to see if they are relevant or helpful in identifying issues. Simply becoming aware of some aspect of how a creative challenge works can sometimes be enough to transcend it. So, the Checklist can help the artist bring possible hidden limitations into the Light. If a creative limitation is difficult to define, you can always make up a name for it - as long it *serves you* in reclaiming your creative energy. You may have words or descriptions of your own to add to the checklists.

3 THINGS TO REMEMBER ABOUT CREATIVE OBSTACLES

- Remember to use the information about Creative Obstacles for your own learning and transformation, and never to judge yourself or anyone else.

- Recognizing, observing, or understanding the nature of a Creative Obstacle can be the first step in transforming it into greater artistic ability and authenticity.

- Creative fear, blocks, and other difficulties represent the artist's trapped creative energy that can be transformed, reclaimed, and redirected into better and more authentic art.

TWO CAUTIONS FOR USING PART II OF THE MASTER ARTIST WITHIN

CAUTION #1: Please do not use the information in Part II chapter to judge yourself. Please do not use it to judge or "fix" anyone else. And please do not use it like a medical journal that tempts one to suddenly imagine all kinds of symptoms when reading about diseases. Again, it is best to maintain a sense of humor about our creative difficulties. A tremendous amount of creative energy goes into the creation of a Creative Obstacle, so try to see each obstacle as a "package of energy" that can be turned around to *benefit* the artist, never to judge. Please use this information to your advantage by bringing the light of your awareness to areas of potential artistic growth. You can go to Part III to begin the process of transforming creative difficulties into better art.

CAUTION #2: Investigating one's own creative blocks or limitations can lead to some pretty powerful feelings, awareness, or memories at times. If you ever find yourself mentally or emotionally "in over your head" when facing creative issues, please search for capable professional help. (See References) Whether a friend, counselor, or doctor, it is good and wise to have the help of a compassionate heart when treading dark waters. Regardless of what you think or feel when addressing a creative difficulty, remember to keep yourself and those around you safe, healthy, and well cared for.

"The hurt you embrace becomes joy. Call it to your arms where it can change."

Jalal ad-Din Muhammed Rumi, Persian poet, 13th C.

"The Perfectionist" (detail) 1936, by Grant Wood. Crayon, gouache, charcoal, and ink on paper, 20" x 16", collection of The Fine Arts Museums, San Francisco, California

6

THE CREATIVE LIMITATIONS OF JUDGING AND BLAMING

One of the biggest drains on a creative person's artistic ability is the very human pastime of "judging" and "blaming." It can be the easiest habit in the world to fall into and require great determination to overcome. But if the artist or creative person would like to create from their inner Master Artist, it helps to let go of the temptation to judge or to place blame. Here's why: The state of mind that invests creative energy in judging or finding fault operates at a different frequency than genius, mastery, or enthusiasm.

Judging, blaming, resenting, and holding contempt are all understandable... life is complicated, and some pretty horrible things have happened in the world. It is so much a part of society, that mutual judging often serves as the basis for friendships, making some people feel bonded or significant. Blaming other people for our creative limitations can provide a good excuse for not being the artist that we wish we could be. Some people, and even whole groups of people, get their sense of identity from what they judge, and who they blame. But the truth is that judging and blaming are ultimately *disempowering* for any artist or creative team.

Judgements are not independent entities in the environment. We create them. We might find reasons or justifications to judge our self, our work, other people, the world, our God, the weather - the possibilities are endless. We might blame society, our family, our karma, life experiences, our own weaknesses, and even the stars for our creative failings. Judging and blaming can be used as just another type of "busy work" - producing nothing, like the dog chasing its tail. There will never be a shortage of reasons to judge in life. We will never run out of people to blame for our artistic shortcomings. We will never come to the end of opportunities to hold contempt.

But, as artists and creative people, we can decide to sacrifice such thoughts and feelings in order to "upgrade" to something better. The ultimate result of judging and blaming is always the same - our creative energy is *influenced* and *directed* by a disempowered state of mind, and thus limits our creative powers.

There is another reason for artists to let go of blaming: As long as we blame another for our Creative Obstacles, we give them *ownership* over that obstacle. Even if we have "proof" that someone or something caused our creative limitations, blaming them can cripple our creativity. If someone or something else *owns* our creative limitation, we are not in the best position to transform that limitation. But once we decide to sacrifice the assignment of blame to another - regardless of how justified - we become the *owners* of our own creative issues. Once we decide to "own" all of our creative issues, we then have the ability, power, and authority to transform them and reclaim our creative energy. As soon as the temptation to blame someone or something creeps back into our consciousness, we can immediately use the Art of Forgiveness (page 185) to let go of everything connected to the creative challenge at hand. Ultimately, any justification for blame becomes far less important to our artistic ability than the inner creative freedom gained through forgiveness and letting go.

Sometimes, we judge and blame ourselves. *Self*-judgment often takes the form of feelings like *shame*, *guilt*, *regret*, and *unworthiness*. Such feelings, whether acknowledged or hidden, are just other forms of judgment that can sabotage an artist's work. Whether shame or guilt is self-generated, or imposed on us by another, the effect on our creativity is oppressive. There have been whole religious schools of thought that have taught innocent little children that they were "born in sin," and that their bodies were something to be ashamed of. For centuries, shame and guilt have been effective tools for controlling and manipulating people. With Forgiveness, creators have the power to transcend all the sources of ignorance and misinformation that have historically promoted shame, guilt, unworthiness, and self judgement. As artists, we have the creative authority to love, heal, embrace, and reclaim all the parts of ourselves.

We might judge our current artistic ability, judge our lack of training, judge experiences from our past, judge the compromise our values, or any number of circumstances. We might judge ourselves over a seeming failure, or a lack of resources, or when comparing our work to another artist's work. We can make a creative decision to let go of all judgements as we become aware of them, which will naturally improve the quality of our creative work. The creative energy that we use to judge ourselves can be transformed into respect, appreciation, gratitude, compassion, and enthusiasm.

Artists who have been victims of crimes often feel shame about being a victim, having thoughts like, "There must be something wrong with me for this to happen." Sometimes, horrible things happen to good and innocent people. For the creative person who feels burdened by tragedy, the ability and willingness to Forgive such life experience is empowering.

If we have guilt or shame after being unkind or dishonest with another, we can forgive our actions, do our best to correct our mistake, and strive to do better. Step one is to acknowledge the action. Step two is to begin the process of *transforming the energy* of guilt to reclaim your creative clarity. Step three is to decide how we would like to treat others in the future.

The Art of Forgiveness can be practiced immediately - anytime, anywhere, out loud, or silently. Nurturing your Sense of Humor can be surprisingly empowering. And learning to cultivate compassion for yourself and others will go a long way to protect you from unnecessary negativity.

Another tricky type of judgment that can sabotage creativity is "self-righteousness." Righteousness is so seductive - it tells us that we are right, or superior, or smarter, and everyone else is wrong. When there is a particularly *righteous* feeling behind a judgment, it becomes especially hard to let go of it. If the target of our self-righteousness is truly harmful or bad, it can feel like a real compromise of our values to Forgive, or to Let Go of our righteousness. But all art begins inside of the artist. If we are *holding on* to the energy of judgment it affects our inner world, which affects our creative work. This winds up giving the target of our judgment or righteousness control over our state of being, and control over our art. The trick is to do our part to creatively improve what truly needs correcting in the world - without the energy of judgment or righteousness manipulating or draining our creative energy.

Judgments can have many different faces. They can look like opinions, fears, regret, righteousness, prejudice, attitudes, unworthiness, self-doubt, resentment, and other experiences that all boil down to a judgment about something or someone - including ourselves. We, as artists and creators, do have a right to reclaim our creative energy and do something better with it. When we become really tired of having our creative works influenced by judgments, we might declare, "Regardless of the reason, proof, situation, or justification, I forgive all of my judgments in order to create better work, and a better world."

We start where we can. For example, an author might have "writer's block" because he is too upset. His behind was bitten by a stray dog last week, and he can hardly sit down. The writer has a very good reason to be angry and blame the dog. He has proof, and the judgment is quite justified. So, instead of writing his book, he is using all of his creativity to plot revenge against the dog. But all of the proof, righteousness, and judgments about the dog will not help him write his book with the quality he would like. In his inner world, there is a "disturbance in the force." But... the writer has options. He has the power to reclaim his creative energy. He can decide to forgive the whole thing - and claim his sore behind as his *own experience*. Once the experience is forgiven, the writer can reclaim his creative energy. The writer's focus is no longer bound by all the anger, judging, and blaming, and his creativity is no longer influenced and controlled by a dog. (We'll forgo jokes about turning the other cheek.)

Another tricky aspect of a judgment is that it always comes back around to "bite us on the butt." How we judge others is often a secret code for the judgments that we hold against ourselves. I have long seen

Luke's passage in the bible as a basic primer on quantum physics, explaining how the energy that we project helps to create our reality, and our creative work: "Do not judge, or you too will be judged. Do not condemn, and you will not be condemned. Forgive, and you will be forgiven. Give, and it will be given to you... For with the measure you use, it will be measured to you..." I am not a big fan of quoting biblical verses, but I have found this dynamic to be pretty consistently true.

Of course, Forgiveness does not mean that we allow ourselves to be harmed or taken advantage of. If there is something or someone harmful in the environment, be responsible and take care of yourself and your loved ones.

When an artist's state of mind is free from the burdens of judging and blaming, there is more room for the inner genius to create. Again, the "judging state of mind" produces a *different frequency* than the "Master Artist state of mind." We can choose to make peace, healing, and creativity more important than revenge. Artists, and even whole nations, can reclaim much of their power and creative energy each and every time we open our hearts and let go of another judgment for the sake of greater possibilities.

3 THINGS TO REMEMBER ABOUT JUDGEMENTS

- Judgements and blame disempower our creative ability, regardless of reason, proof, or justification.

- Forgiveness can immediately cut the chains of judgement and blaming so that artists can reclaim their creative energy.

- Artistic genius and mastery operate at a different frequency than blame, contempt, judgements, or self-righteousness.

I see my own personal "Judgment Dragon" as shiny and seductive, whispering in my ear about all the good and righteous reasons for judging something or blaming someone. He tells me, "It feels so good to be right, and make everyone else wrong, and you don't have to be responsible for any of it." When he sneaks into my mind, I immediately start practicing the Art of Forgiveness, remember my Sense of Humor, and use the Art of Letting Go to tame my Dragon - remembering that I have far better things to do with my creative energy.

"I would permit no man, no matter what his colour might be, to narrow and degrade my soul by making me hate him."

Writer, speaker, and educator Booker T. Washington 1856-1915

CHECKLIST FOR BLAME AND JUDGEMENTS:

Self judgement

Shame or guilt

Unworthiness

Self-righteousness

Resentment

Prejudice

Contempt

Hate

Blame

Family members or friends

Our education, or lack thereof

Family heritage or history

Bullies, attackers, abusers, and mean people

Childhood experiences

Discrimination issues

Current society, culture, or people

World leaders or officials

Social status or wealth

Current trends in the art world

The world, or world history

Superior/inferior complex

God, or higher power

The art world, publishers, movie studios

Current news, media, or technology

Life experience

Other people's differences

My creative work, or lack thereof

Relationships, or lack thereof

Other:

"Ophelia by the Pond," 1894, by John William Waterhouse. Oil on canvas, 49" x 29" Private collection.

7

LIMITING OPINIONS THAT SABOTAGE CREATIVITY

An opinion can be described as a self-created attitude or point of view. A Limiting Opinion is a rigid position that can block an artist from creating or seeing possibilities *beyond* the dictates of that opinion. This can be either an artist's own opinion, or a concern about someone else's opinion. When does a Limiting Opinion become a Creative Block? When that opinion compromises, influences, or blocks an artist's ability to do their best and most original creative work.

There are two kinds of opinions that can sabotage an artist's creative ability. The most sabotaging Limiting Opinion is worshipping the opinions of other people. This includes the opinions of organizations, art publications, social media, and art theories. The art world, in particular, is full of opinions. When we are concerned about the opinions of others, we are giving some of our creative power over to other people. It is difficult for artists to be loyal to both their inner creative genius, and the opinions of other people at the same time. We all want to be liked, but when we try too hard to please others, it can sabotage the quality of our work and block us from creative Inspiration.

The second kind of Limiting Opinion can be our *own* fixed positions that keeps us from growing as an artist or creator. Sometimes we create our own Limiting Opinions, and sometimes they are adopted from other artists, past education, media sources, organizations, current fashion, and people with an agenda to sell. A fixed opinion can keep us from evolving as artists because they tell us the we *already know everything*. Your inner Master Artist transcends rigid opinions, creating original work that surpasses limiting points of view.

When an artist is burdened by a concern about what others think, it becomes difficult to be authentic in their expression. The all-mighty "God of Opinion" demands loyalty, and can be one of the most subtle and notorious of all Creative Obstacles. Whether the artist is investing their creative energy into maintaining a certain image - or compromising their work to please others - a preoccupation with how others see us becomes a limitation. The state of mind that is concerned about what others think, and the state of mind that produces original work, operate at different frequencies on our creativity scale. Even though a habit of worshipping opinion can push an artist to produce work, it is usually not the inspiration for our *best* work. When we create according to Limiting Opinions, or what we *think* will impress other people, we are not creating as the inner Master Artist.

3 THINGS TO REMEMBER ABOUT OPINIONS

- Your inner Master Artist, and the source of your creative genius, is not burdened by the opinions of other people.

- Limiting Opinions are often adopted from other artists, social media, art publications, and organizations, and are not compatible with artistic mastery.

- Artists cannot be loyal to both their inner Inspiration, and the opinions of other people at the same time.

The pattern of fearing the opinions of others may even go back to prehistoric times. Once upon a time, if one was a little different from the rest of the tribe, they could be ridiculed, exiled, and maybe even eaten for dinner. It is natural human behavior, and possibly in our DNA to fear what others think. We may even fear the opinions of dead people: "What would my grandfather think of these nude paintings?" As crazy as it sounds, some artists direct their creativity according to a parent, a mentor, a teacher, or an art theory written by someone who is no longer living. As artists, we eventually get to a point where we just have to rebel against the confines of opinions and reclaim our right to create as our True Self. That is where the inner creative genius lives.

Limiting Opinions almost always have a quality of negativity about them, and some even hold an inherent threat. Our own Limiting Opinions about creativity can be so fixed and rigid that they keep us from seeing, learning, hearing, or accepting new ideas. Art institutions, magazines, and websites often cultivate opinions about what is good or bad, valuable or worthless, cool or not cool, profound or trivial, accepted or not accepted. Such Limiting Opinions about art encourage mental positions and theories that may or may not be true. Paradoxically, rigid opinions can also render us easily manipulated by forces that tell us what we want to hear. It is hard to create authentic work or make masterful creative decisions when influenced by commercially produced tastes and opinions. Discovering and staying true to your inner Master Artist - regardless of opinions - is a skill that is worth cultivating.

PLEASING CLIENTS AND PATRONS

Many professional artists, of course, do need to make clients happy, and work with their client's opinions about what they want. To make a living, they need to produce work that that the gallery can sell, write scripts that an audience can understand, and take the needs of other human beings into consideration. Creative people can produce original and authentic work even when serving the needs or preferences of their audience. A strong relationship with our inner Master Artist enables us to put that quality and frequency into any work that we do. Historically, all great works have had to overcome pre-existing opinions about the established rules of their time. According to historians, Michelangelo resisted the job of painting the Sistine Chapel – but he still created something that has awed and inspired people for over 500 years. Maintaining our *inner mastery* results in greater authenticity in our creative projects, regardless of the task at hand.

We must remember that works of creative genius that "stand the test of time" were created by the artists, writers, musicians, and inventors who were doggedly true to themselves - not by ones who depended upon the opinions of other people.

Often, just becoming *aware* that we have been influenced by a Limiting Opinion is enough to start transcending it. Create an effective Guiding Star for yourself. Write in your Secret Journal. Practicing Meditation, The Circle Game, The True Self/False Self Game, and other Tools for the Artists in Part III can also help to keep the artist inwardly strong in the face of Limiting Opinions.

My Dragon of Opinion has a skinny face, with eyes close together, looking down his nose through magnifying spectacles. He has a fat bottom from sitting around all day critiquing everything. His muscles are weak, his scales are soft and flimsy, but his eyes can bore right through an easily intimidated artist. It doesn't work to fight or argue with him, as he has a prefabricated answer for everything. But he loses power in the presence of a bold heart - an artist who is loyal to their True Self. As I strengthen my inner life, love and respect myself, and create the work that I truly love, I become immune to his presence. As I reclaim the power that the Opinion Dragon once held over me, he morphs into creative loyalty, integrity, and determination.

"This above all - to thine own self be true, And it must follow, as night the day, Thou canst not be false to any man."

English playwright, William Shakespeare, *Hamlet* 1:3 1602

CHECKLIST FOR LIMITING OPINIONS:

Wanting to fit in

Wanting approval

Fear of embarrassment

Art theories

Fear of rejection

Concern about legacy

A need for attention

Concern about image

Designing your work to please others

Pleasing professors or art critics

Temptation to compromise work

Fear of what others think

Looking to art publications for answers

Comparing your career to others

Commercially promoted fashion

Competition

Envy or comparison

Unworthiness

Fear of exile, shame, or persecution

"Vertumnus" c.1590, by Italian painter, Giuseppe Arcimboldo. Oil on wood panel, 28" x 23." Portrait of Rudolf II, Holy Roman Empire as the Roman god, Vertumnus. In the collection of the Skokloster Castle, Sweden.

8

CREATIVE CONFUSION

Creative Confusion is what artists might experience when overwhelmed with inner chaos, conflicting directions, or burdened by too many influences. It often has the effect of creating inertia or procrastination. If the artist is avoiding a creative project, the creation of busy work can produce both distraction and confusion. Although periods of *chaos, confusion,* or even *nothingness* can be frustrating, they can be transformed into your next level of artistic ability.

For an artist, being in state of Creative Confusion while trying to work is especially frustrating. "I want to work, but I don't know what to do next." "There are so many complications that I don't know where to start." "I feel like a different person now, and I am tired of my old way of working." These are common thoughts of an artist experiencing Creative Confusion.

Most creative people are happiest when enthusiastically focused on an exciting project, confident in what they are doing. The wonderful thing about being creatively Inspired is that all aspects of the artist's being can work together as one creative force - the mind, the emotions, the body, the imagination, and the spirit all work as a "superhuman team" in the studio. There is no inner struggle or argument. It takes an Inspiring, exciting, and challenging creative vision to get "everyone" inside the artist going in the same direction at the same time.

But, when creative people feel pulled between several different projects, concerns, motivations, and responsibilities - all with competing goals, desires, and agendas, it can be difficult to make decisions. Inner struggles between strongly held beliefs, the world's demands, and what the inner Master Artist wants to create can result in Creative Confusion.

Here are 5 possible sources of Creative Confusion:

- Conflicting motivations
- Transitional periods
- Inside interference
- Outside interference
- Poor health

Conflicting motivations cause Creative Confusion when an artist is trying to focus their energy in too many directions at one time. For example, I have often felt pulled between painting portraits, paintings of the natural world, and going on hiking adventures to paint outdoors. Often such indecision is fueled by different agendas that have nothing to do with true inner Inspiration. When an artist is going from project to project, trying to be all things to all people, confusion can creep in. Maybe we *can* do everything, but not all at the same time. Most creative people also need time for family and friends, time to explore new things, time to take care of themselves, and time to create financial security - all in addition to their creative work. In truth, all these parts of life are interconnected and support each other - but the clarity to decide what to focus on at any given time can be a challenge, especially in a demanding and complicated world. It becomes vitally important to discover what is *most important* to you as an artist in order know where to place your energy. As loyalty to your True Self becomes stronger, it becomes easier to let go of lesser agendas, and easier to Let Go of things that might sabotage your inner creative direction.

Transitional periods happen when an artist goes through periods of feeling lost or confused because of personal growth or change. For example, a creative person might be very comfortable with their normal way of doing things, only to have that familiarity shaken by inner growth or transformation. Sometimes artists have a genuinely life-changing experience, rendering old motivations or truths no longer as meaningful as they once were. The artist may be Inspired to expand into a new way of creating, or a new way of seeing things. But such changes rarely happen instantly. Usually, the creative person will experience a "blank space," or a "void," that stands between the *old* way of being, and the *new* way of creating. During such transitional periods, the sense of "nothingness" can be disorienting. In Chapter 12, this experience is called the "Sea of Transition". Although the Sea of Transition is listed as a Creative Obstacle, it is not necessarily a creative problem. But, artists usually *experience it* as a problem. Transition periods can feel like confusion, or like being lost, but they are actually more like a *bridge* between two places. Crossing this transitional bridge is a common experience for many creative people. While treading water in the Sea of Transition, it is important for the artist to maintain self-respect, and continue excellent self-care while working to gain a new clarity. When the new "level" of creative clarity and Inspiration blossoms, the artist will need to be in great shape to meet the challenge. Traversing a creative void is also a great time to go on an adventure, learn something new, strengthen our skills, do some volunteer work, or help someone in need - anything that strengthens and expands the artist's inner experience also tends to strengthen their art.

Inside Interference is often the result of a very creative person trying to *withhold* their creativity, avoid a creative issue, or create below their level of artistic ability. Such a suppression of creative energy can create a lot of inner noise and confusion because that unused energy *will* manifest as something. If the artist is not using their creative energy to create with the best of their ability, the unused energy might manifest as an overload of thoughts, concerns, habits, or emotions. A conflicted artist might create so much busy work that they find themselves in complete overwhelm, and unable to accomplish anything in the studio. Secret Agendas that fight against what the inner artist wants to create can produce mental and emotional confusion, scattering the artist's energy. Unresolved judgements or feelings can also confuse your creative focus and influence your work. Artists are multidimensional and creative beings - to keep all of our inner dimensions working together in harmony, it helps to know our True Self very well.

Outside Interference is any outside energy that can produce confusion for an artist, interfere with their mental clarity, or compromise their creative work. This can be anything from listening to too many news reports to a crazy-making person trying to interfere with your work. The energy of some people might have a disrupting effect on the artist. Performing artists might experience all kinds of confusion-causing energy projected towards them. (See Ch. 17) Trying to work in an environment with people who project words or energy disrupting to your work can produce Creative Confusion. Certain kinds of music or sound can be inspiring or supportive in the studio - but, some sounds can be so distracting or oppressive that they make focus or enthusiasm impossible. If you are an artist experiencing Outside Interference, you may need to protect your creative process by making your studio a "sanctuary" that is free of unwanted physical, non-physical, or psychic disturbances. Try imagining a cloud of protective light or well-being around you and your work space. Artists can cultivate a "master's state of mind," and protect their work environment from sabotaging influences when creating.

Poor Health - the kind that causes Creative Confusion, can look like a variety of circumstances: High or low blood sugar, high or low blood pressure, insomnia, an infection in the body, inadequate circulation, too much alcohol or caffeine, poor nutrition, sinus or inner ear issues, heavy metals in the body, and toxins in the environment. All art begins with the artist, so it is vital to take good care of the artist. Unused creative energy can also physically "back up" on creative people, resulting in health issues that cause more confusion. Artists experiencing such symptoms need to focus on creating better health to feel stronger, have more energy, and think more clearly. Remember that the brain needs oxygen, and the body needs movement to be strong, healthy, and eliminate waste. Your blood needs to circulate to deliver nutrients to your brain. If you think that poor health is possibly creating Creative Confusion, and you can't identify the problem yourself, get help right away by visiting a good doctor, chiropractor, wholistic practitioner, or even a free clinic.

    We should not allow periods of Creative Confusion to become so familiar that they become a kind of "comfort zone" of inertia. If you are experiencing confusion more often than not, ask yourself if it is perhaps self-created in order to avoid your creative challenges. Creative Confusion can be self-manufactured when an artist is fearful of a challenging project or the next step in their career. It takes great courage to create something new and dynamic, and a state of confusion can serve as an effective way to hide from our fears and limitations. For most artists, periods of confusion are always temporary. *Never, never, ever* allow Creative Confusion to become a habit, a place to hide your gifts, or use it as a reason to do anything unhealthy or harmful to yourself.

3 THINGS TO REMEMBER ABOUT CREATIVE CONFUSION

- Creative Confusion happens when the artist has too many conflicting desires, beliefs, concerns, motivations, agendas, or outer influences.

- Never allow Creative Confusion to become a habit, a comfort zone of inertia, or a way to avoid your creative challenges.

- If the artist's mind, emotions, spirit, body, and imagination are not all working together as a "creative team," there may be inner disagreements that need to be resolved.

How do we transform a period of Creative Confusion into creative or artistic mastery? Practicing the Tools for the Artist in Part III can be very effective for addressing different kinds of Creative Confusion. The Foundation Skills for Creative Mastery can go a long way to avoid unnecessary confusion in the first place. The Tools for the Artist are designed to encourage a stronger relationship with your inner Master Artist and the source of your creative genius. Sometimes, the extra oxygen and circulation from a long run or a vigorous hike is enough to transcend confusion. As simple as it sounds, cleaning and organizing your work environment can begin to turn things around. It may help to remove certain things, sounds, images, or people from your work area. Writing for Clarity is often a good first step for turning Creative Confusion into a more clear and Inspired direction. Questioning for Clarity can evoke new answers and can often cut through confusion. The Circle Game is helpful for immediate clarity when feeling lost or stuck in the middle of a project due to too many considerations.

My "Confusion Dragon" is shape-shifting, and usually swirls around my head like a cloud when he visits. He can make me feel either lethargic or panicky. It takes a lot of creative energy to maintain confusion, so this Dragon holds a lot of energy that can be reclaimed and redirected. He might trick me into adding all kinds of activities and projects to my schedule, producing mental overwhelm. He feeds on inertia. So, a good long run on the beach can offer immediate relief. The Art of Letting Go helps. Having a good Guiding Star to remind me of my ultimate intention as an artist can be handy when the Confusion Dragon shows up. It takes vigilance to keep up with one's ever-evolving inner genius and inner Master Artist in an often demanding and entertaining world.

> "I tell you: one must still have chaos within oneself to give birth to a dancing star"
>
> *Thus Spoke Zarathustra*, 1883-91, Friedrich Nietzsche

CHECKLIST FOR CREATIVE CONFUSION:

Indecision

High or low blood sugar

Inability to focus

Anemia, or health issue

Inadequate nutrition

Insomnia, lack of sleep

Creating overwhelm to avoid work

Distractions from media or people

Trying to be all things to all people

Withholding creative energy

Haunted by secret agendas

Looking for answers from outside of yourself

Listening to too many sources of information

Conflicting beliefs

Misunderstanding

Not allowing time to find the True Self

Concern about what others think

Poor circulation

Needing time to grieve someone

Laziness or inertia

Not enough physical exercise

Lack of mental clarity

Dizziness or exhaustion

Too much alcohol or caffeine

Unresolved emotions

Toxins in the environment

Needing time for introspection

Another's psychic energy

"Ellen Terry as Shakespeare's Lady Macbeth" (detail) 1889, by American painter, John Singer Sargent. Oil on canvas, 87" x 45" In the collection of the Tate Gallery, London, England.

9

SECRET AGENDAS THAT LIMIT CREATIVITY

Any artist who wants to create authentic and masterful work, needs the creative freedom to listen to the voice of their True Self. Having a Secret Agenda, however, could sabotage an artist's creative freedom. A normal agenda can be a plan or a to-do list that helps you to accomplish something. A Secret Agenda, however, is a hidden motivation that can sabotage the genius or originality of an artist's work. Such a Secret Agenda might be a private need to impress someone, a desire to control a situation, wanting to project a certain image, or trying to promote an ideology or belief system. It forces the artist to choose between following their own authentic voice, or following the interests of the agenda. It is said that "One cannot have two masters." To create art with mastery and authenticity, we must be *loyal* to our inner Master Artist and the source of our creative genius.

A Secret Agenda acts as a Creative Obstacle because it enslaves the creativity of the artist. It *undermines* any idea or Inspiration that does not serve the agenda's mission. Secret Agendas are created out of fear, a sense of lack, a fear of inferiority, or a fear of losing control - they often want something from the world at large. Limiting agendas are usually not motivated by love, generosity, confidence, or creativity. The source of your creative genius produces truth, Inspiration, enthusiasm, and original ideas. It will not be on the same wavelength or frequency as any Secret Agenda.

There is a big difference between an *intention* and a Secret Agenda - although sometimes it can be tricky to tell the difference. The two are *energetically* different, and *feel* different. A clearly defined *intention* is energizing and clarifying. An clear intention can protect us from being sidetracked, providing a sense of direction and determination. Secret Agendas, however, are disempowering and are usually a burden to the creative process.

For example, if we have an *intention* to create a beautiful mosaic, our inner artist guides us to make the best choices in color, tile, design, and materials along the way. If, on the other hand, we have a Secret Agenda to only use materials from a particular company because they have a cute salesperson, that *imposed limitation* can block what the inner genius, and the inner Master Artist might create. A good intention allows us the *freedom* to choose what is best in any given moment.

A Secret Agenda becomes a creative limitation because it demands that we bend our creativity to its will. Even the most noble of Secret Agendas can act as a creative limitation because they are limited by what the mind understands. The inner Master Artist can access Inspiration and ideas from the "Unknown World" of creativity, producing extraordinary work *beyond* what the mind currently thinks is possible.

Another Secret Agenda has a financial motivation. I have seen students excited about learning a new art form or skill - only to have that enthusiasm and love of learning compromised by the questions like, "What is this worth?" or "How can I start making money with this?" The new artist's focus might then switch from creating from their heart, to creating what they think someone else would buy. Switching one's attention from their inner voice to fulfill the agenda of profit can make it difficult to access Inspiration or creative genius.

A creative person may have spent years trying to cultivate a certain image that they would like to project out into the world. Protecting that self-image can become a limiting Secret Agenda if the artist allows it. If a new, original, and dynamic idea should come forward, that new idea may be severely edited, or dismissed altogether, if it is not compatible with their highly valued self-image. All self-images fade with time, whereas a timeless new idea or work of art could live much longer.

Some artists have been advised to create a *brand* for their creative work in order to be more professional or successful. A *brand* is like a public image that is supposed to make an artist's work more famous, recognizable, or memorable to potential media outlets or customers. The problem is that limiting one's creative identity to a *brand* can become a creative limitation. As with a Secret Agenda, true Inspiration might be edited, corrupted, or dismissed if the new Inspiration does not fit into the *brand*. Of course, companies and professional artists need to create financial success, especially if they have a family to support. But all agendas must be checked at the door of the studio when the artist wants to follow their own inner voice and creative genius.

Financial pressures and responsibilities make it difficult for most artists to create without the agenda of "profitability" hanging around the studio. Maybe your inner Master Artist loves thinking about cash flow, but mine unfortunately, couldn't care less. Being a brilliant inventor, designer, musician, writer, or other artist is a calling - and it does not come with a guarantee that anyone will recognize your work enough to give you lots of money for it. Master Artists are willing to create good work in any circumstance, with the situation at hand. If you find it difficult to create original and brilliant work while trying to be profitable, there may be times to do other work for financial security, while maintaining creative freedom in the studio. Many brilliant people throughout history have had "side jobs." Celebrate and be grateful if you are lucky enough to be financially supported while doing your best and most authentic work - and celebrate anyway if you have a day job that allows you to be an artist

.

3 THINGS TO REMEMBER ABOUT SECRET AGENDAS

- Secret Agendas enslave an artist's creativity by dismissing any Inspiration or new idea that does not serve its hidden mission.

- Your inner Master Artist can produce work far superior to any reward promised by a Secret Agenda.

- Artists can access Inspiration and original ideas from the Unknown Worlds of creativity, beyond what the mind can understand.

My Secret Agenda Dragon is sneaky - it has a slippery body, squinty eyes, and a tiny head. I feel the weight of it on my shoulders and my chest, and it drains my energy if I let him. I find that when I am meditating, and lifting up into my higher self, the demands of the agenda melt away, allowing me to see them as the illusions and limitations that they are.

Meditation, the True Self/False Self Game, and other Tools for the Artist in Part III can help creative people to gain clarity about their creative work. The Art of Forgiveness can transform agendas like revenge, competition, or vindication. The Art of Letting Go can help artists to sacrifice agendas that would sabotage the quality of their work, and reclaim their valuable creative energy.

"There is something bigger and better and more worthwhile than the things we see about us, the things we live by and strive for. There is an Undiscovered Beauty, a Divine Excellence, just beyond us. Let us stand on tiptoe, forgetting the meaner things, and grasp of it what we may. If the Palace of Fine Arts is any kind of success, it must say something like that to the people who see it."

Architect, Bernard Maybeck, *Sunset Pacific Monthly*, 1915

CHECKLIST FOR SECRET AGENDAS:

Trying to create or maintain an image

Upholding a belief system

Wanting to be famous, or like another artist

Trying to impress or outshine someone

Wanting revenge or justice

Loyalty to an organization

Concern about how much things cost

Control or manipulation

Misplaced loyalty

Wanting vindication

Wanting recognition or fame

Expecting your art to fit into a brand or style

Protecting a weakness

Wanting to promote a political of religious belief

Overriding inspiration with profitability issues

Fear of rejection or exile

An attachment to being right about something

Wanting approval from someone

Concern about what history will say about you

Believing in another's art theory

Wanting to fit in

Wanting to hide something

Promoting a school of thought

Wanting something from someone

Fulfilling a past vow

Wanting respect or admiration

Competition

Trying to prove something

"At Merlin's feet the wily Vivian lay." (detail) 1860's, by Gustave Dore. One of many steel engravings made to illustrate Alfred, Lord Tennyson's book of poems, *Idylls of the King*.

10

CONTROL AND MANIPULATION AS CREATIVE OBSTACLES

Artists who are also parents, teachers, spouses, coaches, and friends often fall into the trap of controlling or manipulating other people. It is easy to avoid facing one's own creative fears, doubts, and inadequacies if one is busy "helping" other people to be their best. The world *is* a better place when we love, help, care, teach, support, and encourage each other. We actually *strengthen* our creative powers by being of service because it helps us to identify with the best part of ourselves. But often, there can be *fine line* between *caring* and *control*, and between *helping* and *manipulation*. Energetically, they feel different. Caring for others can empower our creative work. Control and manipulation can sabotage our art - or - help us to avoid our creative work all together.

For some creators, improving the lives of other people or the environment *is* their creative mastery and authenticity at work. It is when we try to micro manage others as a way to *avoid* the challenges of our own highest and best creative expression that it becomes a creative block.

Our inner Master Artist is not interested in controlling or manipulating anyone - it has better things to do. Yet, a habit of trying to control is not an uncommon challenge for many creative people. The best way to affect change in the world around us is by being the best person, and the best creator that we can be.

When a creative person is not using their creative energy *to the degree that they are capable*, that creative energy can "back up" and come out in different ways - sometimes creating situations that we don't want. Just like squeezing a ball of clay until it seeps out through the fingers, the creative energy might take a variety of shapes. One shape that unused or misdirected creative energy can take is trying to live through other people, organizations, or situations.

The paradox is that when we step out of bounds to micromanage the life of another, it rarely brings us a lot of love, admiration, or loyalty. And it does nothing for the quality of our creative work. When in a habit of controlling, we might feel like we do so much for others only to wonder why we are taken for granted and unappreciated. It is difficult to appreciate anyone's generosity or caring when feeling controlled or manipulated. Creative people find that when we are putting our love and energy into work that we find genuinely challenging and fulfilling, we don't have the time to control anyone or anything else.

The story of a certain failed artist who felt rejected is well known: Rather than overcome his creative obstacles, he went on to control and manipulate a whole country into blaming and persecuting certain groups of people, dragging most of the world into war. Perhaps the best thing that he created was a perfect example of what it looks like to control and manipulate - and - what it looks like when we allow someone else to control, manipulate, and influence our lives.

Once an artist starts to create work that is both fulfilling and challenging, they find that the need to control, manipulate, and micromanage the world around them starts to fade away. Ultimately, the urge to control or manipulate is based on some kind of fear. Sometimes the fear is known, and sometimes unknown. The secret voice of Control might sound like, "If I don't control this situation, something horrible is going to happen." Or, "If I fix this person out of the goodness of my heart, it will make up for all my failures." Or, "As long as I am the hero, I will be loved, valued, and accepted." Or, "I'll never be the artist that I wanted to be, so I'll just experience it through them."

I understand the temptation to control. When I teach portrait painting classes, I often have to fight the impulse to take the brush out of a student's hand in order to "fix" the portrait they are working on. I call this "backseat painting," and it's not a good way for a student to learn or gain confidence. (It's embarrassing when I catch myself doing this.)

As a mother, I know that stopping the temptation to control can be very difficult. We want only the best for our kids, and we can't stand the thought of them suffering the slings and arrows of life. We don't want them to experience pain and heartache. But, we learn to see and trust the Spirit in them. We respect that they, too, have their own inner creative genius and abilities beyond our imagining. When loyal to our True Self and engaged in work we feel Inspired and called to do, we become role models for our children and the world without even trying.

3 THINGS TO REMEMBER ABOUT CONTROL AND MANIPULATION

- Control or manipulation is usually a way to avoid what we truly want to be creating, and the challenges we may face.

- When we are creating to the best of our ability, we have a greater effect on the world than any amount of control or manipulation.

- Other people can never be our "work of art" - they have their own inner creative genius and inner Master Artist.

My Control Dragon looks like a sweet and friendly intellectual, but with sharp teeth and claws that he knows how to flash at just the right time. He is fast, with a long and flexible body and many arms capable of juggling many things at one time. Being full of creative energy, he has a righteous justification for everything he does, and has proof for every theory. He knows my deepest creative fears, and whispers in my ear the stories of just how perfect the world could be if I would just let him fix it all. He has a table full of charts, scrolls, and plans for how to rule the world, if I would only ignore my beautiful work and follow him. The more I believe the illusions of the Control Dragon, the stronger he grows. But, as I see through his illusions, I am able to reclaim the creative energy that he tricked me into giving him. The more time I spend in the studio creating work that I love, the more he turns into the determination that I need in the studio. I find that practicing A Healthy Sense of Humor, The Art of Letting Go, and challenging myself with work that I love keeps the Control Dragon under control.

> "Like an artist with no art form, she became dangerous."
>
> Writer, Toni Morrison, *Sula* 1973

CHECKLIST FOR PATTERNS OF CONTROL AND MANIPULATION:

Micro managing other people

Avoiding creative work

Opinions about how others should behave

Proselytizing or preaching

Allowing self-image to override inspiration

Overcompensation

Avoiding creative work by over-concern for others

Attachment to comfort zone

Requiring others to see things your way

Disrespect for others point of view

Withholding creativity if conditions are not just right

Manipulation by withholding kindness or approval

Fear of facing creative obstacles

Constantly correcting others

Over-responsibility

Wanting to feel important

Feeling easily hurt or threatened

Doing your child's work

Doing your student's work

Inability to trust others

Disrespect for how others do things

Being a bully

Intimidating or undermining others

Using anger or yelling to control the environment

Withholding creativity

Critiquing instead of creating

"Bacchus" c1595, by Italian painter, Caravaggio (Michelangelo Mersi da Caravaggio.)   Oil on canvas, about 37" x 33" In the collection of the Galleria degli Uffizi in Florence, Italy.

11

HABITS AND ADDICTIONS THAT BURDEN THE ARTIST

This chapter is especially important for artists, students, and creative people who might be vulnerable to harmful habits when faced with the unique challenges of a creative life. With greater understanding and awareness, perhaps fewer people will turn to this type of self-sabotage.

Historically, there have been many creative people who have fallen into the trap of substance abuse and self-harm. Addictions and sabotaging habits become blocks, limitations, and obstacles because they interfere with an artist's ability to do their best work. It takes a tremendous amount of an artist's energy to create and maintain an addiction. Overcoming and transforming an addiction enables the artist to *reclaim* and *redirect* all that lost creativity back into their art and their life. In this chapter, we will look at some of the reasons *why* it is so easy for some creative people to look for comfort, escape, or inspiration through substance abuse. The hope is that with a greater understanding of *why* a creative person would choose to create an addiction, it will be easier to make more empowering choices.

All kinds of people fall into a life choice of habit or addiction. Here are a few of the causes, reasons, or situations that artists, in particular, might find themselves vulnerable:

The Vulnerable Heart: Unlike other professions, artists often put the deepest and most personal aspect of *who they are* into their work. So, when other people judge and evaluate their work, it feels like they are judging and evaluating the very heart of the artist who created it. Performing artists, especially, can feel very exposed and vulnerable when the world's judgements, attachments, projections, and other types of energy start coming at them. Alternately, rejection or disinterest from an audience can be translated as worthlessness. Some artists are uncomfortable with success, and, might be tempted to numb that discomfort with substances or harmful habits. Professional critics make a living by evaluating things they may not even understand. The public can have unreasonable expectations. Oddly, being talented, beautiful, or even just "lucky" is enough to invite cruelty or resentment from both friends and total strangers.

If the artist is feeling "vampired", threatened, ridiculed, misunderstood, or overly exposed, the escape promised by substance abuse might be very tempting. But in the end, this kind of escape will only wind up sabotaging the artist and compromising their creative work. Addiction will always betray the artist and let them down. If you are an artist feeling overly sensitive or vulnerable, it is time to build the inner strength required to manage a broader range of situations. Practice the fine art of not taking things personally. Develop strength in your body. Take enough time in nature or travel to recharge your energy. Upgrade how well you take care of your inner life, and how wisely you choose your friends.

The courage to take risks: Working artists are often not happy when limiting themselves to the safety of the status quo. They want to grow, takes risks, and create work that transcends what they did the year before. In order to access their inner creative genius, the artist must reach *beyond* the safety of the Known World. But leaving familiar ground can often feel scary, lonely, and insecure. When traversing the Unknown Worlds of creativity, there are few guarantees or reference points, but plenty of risks. The risks involved in producing something new can range from ecstatic to gut-wrenching. Most great or Inspired works of art were created with some kind of risk taken by an artist or creative team.

Unfortunately, many creative people have turned to substance abuse for temporary comfort or false courage when facing a creative risk – only to find an addiction sabotaging the very work they so love. The exercises in Part III can help to transform the insecurity of creative risk into enthusiasm. To manage the doubt and alienation involved in creative risk, it is helpful to make time for friends, family, self-care, inner attunement, and interests beyond the studio.

Managing extreme emotions: Gifted artists often have a *so much* creative energy that their actions, feelings, or expression can seem *more extreme*. Emotions can seem more extreme. Their sense of humor can be more extreme. Creative projects can sound more extreme. Perceptions and reactions can be more extreme. A heightened sense of perception can help the artist to produced extraordinary work, but also render them more vulnerable to depression. There is such a "natural high" that is experienced when creating in the "Master Artist Zone," and it can be difficult to return to the "ordinary life" of being a mere mortal when the work is over.

If you are a high-energy artist working passionately on a project, it may feel awkward to even talk to people who are not involved with the creative process. Supposedly, Ernest Hemingway would drink "to make other people more interesting." My father was a very accomplished jazz musician, and he had difficulty relating to anyone other than dogs and other jazz musicians. He also had a hard time returning to the "regular world" after a performance without getting high. But ultimately, substance abuse had a negative effect on his music career - the very thing he most loved. It took many difficult experiences before he decided that his health and relationships were more important to him. It is vital for artists and creative people to learn how to own, embrace, and become comfortable with the extreme feelings that occasionally come with a creative life.

Looking for Inspiration: As hard-working artists, we depend on our source of Inspiration to create engaging work. Thus, it can be depressing, or even frightening, during periods when our creative Inspiration seems to disappear. We may wonder *who we are* when we suddenly have nothing to say. As natural as it is to have "quiet times" between bursts of creative output, it can feel like the end of the world when our Inspiration moves on without telling us where it went. It might be easy to imagine that if we use a mind-altering substance, it could "jump start" some Inspiration. Or perhaps the right substance will give us courage, make us smarter, or dispel our creative fears. After all, many cultures have used substances to embark on "vision quests," speak to spirits, or find answers to life's mysteries. But for the artist, looking for answers through substance abuse will always just create more obstacles rather than guidance or Inspiration.

All art begins within the artist - not with a substance or habit that disperses creative energy. Inspiration comes through the artist's *inner world*. The source of creative genius is *inside* the artist. Original creations begin *inside* the creative person. Learn to appreciate the quiet times and make good use of them. Opening the door to creative Inspiration can be found through Meditation, travel, moving out in nature, helping others in need, or other actions that can expand one's *inner life*. Just as Olympic athletes must do *far more* than the average person in order to accomplish great feats, an artist working at a high level of creativity must work towards inner mastery in a way that is *beyond* ordinary life.

Looking for comfort: Artists and creators often feel *different* from other people. Feeling *different* can result in feelings of doubt, alienation, and insecurity. When deeply involved in a creative project, artists can feel like they live in a "separate reality." And, this is often true. In order to create new, original, and brilliant work, creators must spend periods of time reaching into *new and unknown territory*. Letting go of something familiar in order to create something that never existed before can require great courage. It's easy to lose reference points and feelings of connection after long periods of being alone in the studio. It can feel wonderful when creating artwork at the top of your ability. But afterwards, it can be disorienting when trying to relate to the rest of the world. During such times, it might be tempting to think that drugs and lots of alcohol will provide comfort or friendships. But true friendships and relationships come through genuine connection - and from kindness, honesty, listening, laughing, and communication. Accepting and being comfortable with our differences is a skill that can be learned. Cultivating inner strength, a sense of humor, an open heart, and good friends can all ease the transition between long hours in the studio and one's fellow human beings.

Avoiding Creative Obstacles: When challenged by seemingly impossible creative limitations or obstacles, some artists have turned to substance abuse as a way to avoid facing those challenges. If you are an artist experiencing obstacles such as fear, doubt, unworthiness, uncertainty, or a feeling of inferiority, it may be tempting to think that drugs or alcohol can provide a safe haven. It's easy to think that escaping your current state of mind will make you courageous, more artistic, or even better-looking. But in truth, an addiction can leave an artist feeling worse than ever about their creative ability and their place in the universe. Creating and maintaining an addiction uses up a tremendous amount of an artist's creative energy, time, and resources.

Any substance or habit can provide only a temporary sense of comfort or illusion. However, the *willingness* to face your creative issue is the first step in transforming it into a new level of creative ability. Inwardly transforming your creative issue allows you to reclaim and redirect your creative power, and open the door to genius and Inspiration.

Creating false images: Sometimes, students and creative types might have an idea of how one is supposed look or behave in order to be "a real artist." They may think that they need to be accepted by certain groups of people, dress a certain way, and feel tempted to make compromises in hopes of fitting in. Creating a false image and trying to fit in with certain groups can make one vulnerable to substance abuse or risky behavior. Substance abuse and risky behavior does not make one a better artist, or a more interesting person, and does not strengthen artistic ability. Such choices almost always sabotage the artist and their creative work. Most young artists want to appear "cool." (or whatever the word is now) But there is a *lesser cool* and a *superior cool*. The *lesser cool* is powerless, trying to impress others to uphold a false image. It is always at the mercy of others and their opinions.

Superior cool is confident enough to be authentic, generous enough to be kind, and dedicated enough to become the best artist possible. *Superior cool* does not let substance abuse compromise the quality of one's art, or the well-being of the artist. Ultimately, the strong, independent, and hard-working artists are the ones who wind up serving as role models, while creating the most authentic and enduring work.

Managing fear and anxiety: It's easy for a creative person to fall into the trap of thinking a drug will provide an escape from fear or anxiety. Substance abuse does not provide real vision, Inspiration, escape, answers, friendship, courage, peace, or other comforts. Creative people can face many kinds of fear: Fear of failure. Fear of the unknown. Fear of success. Fear of the public. Fear of the truth. Fear of panic attacks. General fear and anxiety. All such creative fear can actually empower the artist once the *energy* of the fear is transformed using the Tools for the Artist in Part III.

Ultimately, trying to manage fear with substance abuse will just increase the power that the fear has over the artist. Most of our inner fears actually represent a part of us – so hiding from them requires that we deny or disown parts of who we are. Facing and transforming the fear, on the other hand, empowers the artist and their creativity. Just like world-class athletes must build both *inner and outer strength* to be their best, Master Artists find the practices that build the inner and outer strength required to do their best and most authentic work. Learning how to embrace fear will result in greater artistic ability, because it allows the artist to reclaim the creative energy that was once tied up in fear.

Managing trauma: Creative people who have had traumatic experiences in their life might look for the comfort, avoidance, resolution, or freedom promised by substance abuse or sabotaging habits. Such experiences might be childhood trauma, military combat, sexual abuse, losing a loved one, natural disasters, or other overwhelming situations. For creative people, getting past such experiences can be especially difficult *exactly because they are so creative.* An artist's unique ability to hear, feel, visualize, imagine, and recreate scenarios can actually work to keep traumatic experiences alive, and therefore more difficult to transcend. It's easy to understand why an artist plagued by such memories would turn to drugs, alcohol, or unhealthy habits for peace of mind. But the escape found through habits or addictions is temporary at best. They never provide lasting freedom from the trauma and are usually self-sabotaging.

While the exercises in Part III can be very helpful for transforming and transcending the creative limitations created by traumatic events, it is best to find qualified and effective help for issues too sever to address alone. Working with an experienced trained professional can help liberate the artist from the effects of the trauma. (Please see the Reference Section) The good news is that the energy gained by transcending a traumatic event can be creatively empowering for the artist.

3 THINGS TO REMEMBER ABOUT ADDICTIONS

- Habits and substance abuse do not solve creative problems.

- Understanding the causes, reasons, and motivations behind substance abuse can help artists to make more empowering choices.

- Substance abuse can "hijack" the mind of an artist - so it is necessary to find qualified help to overcome an addiction as soon as possible to reclaim and redirect one's creative power.

HABITS VERSUS ADDICTIONS

A *habit* is not always the same thing as an *addiction* - habits can work either *for* or *against* the artist. Habits often represent either something that we like and do repeatedly, or, a comfort zone that was developed over time. There are good habits and not-so-good habits. A habit of walking every morning to get oxygen into your brain can be very beneficial, but a habit of checking in with media every 5 minutes can be sabotaging to the quality of your creative work. Since habits are bound to happen anyway, why not create habits that support your well-being, and help you to produce your best and most authentic work?

When an action, a feeling, or a substance becomes an *addiction*, the artist no longer has the freedom of choice - because the brain, and how it functions, has been *hijacked*. An addicted artist is no longer the "master of their domain," and has handed their power over to something outside of themselves. Addictions become so all-encompassing that a creative person might spend most of their time, resources, and creative energy to maintain that addiction - thus sabotaging their creative work. So if the ritual of doing something repeatedly really works for you, it is best to create good habits that empower your well-being and your creative work.

UNDERSTANDING MOTIVATIONS FOR CREATING HABITS OR ADDICTIONS

There are many types of addictions that can sabotage the work of a creative person, and various motivations behind those addictions. Transforming or transcending the motivation can help the artist to make healthier choices. The following list of causes, reasons, or motivators is provided to help an artist identify and understand potential issues behind various kinds of addiction.

Addictions can take the form of *actions* like gambling, shopping, sex, smoking, pain, pleasure, media, pornography, fantasizing, overeating, or negative thinking. Addiction to *substances* can include alcohol, drugs, stimulants, or food. Whatever the addiction, creative people usually need help from experienced professionals to overcome their issues, and regain their creative independence.

Why would any intelligent artist or creator choose a life of addiction, especially when we live in a time with so much information about the dangers? Many people start out looking for a degree of fun, escape, comfort, comradery, or peace of mind, only to find themselves addicted more easily than expected. Regardless of what anyone tells you, there is no comfort, no thrill, and no experience more important than your creative gifts, and your ability to share them with the world.

Common causes, reasons, and motivations for creating addictions might include:

Trying to quiet the mind

Escaping pain or fear

Trying to find courage

Fear of a larger self

Wanting comfort or pleasure

Impatience with self

Self-medicating to overcome an issue

Shortcut to feeling good

Wanting connection with others

Escaping the pressure of expectations

Fear of failure or rejection

Concern about an image

Feelings of alienation

Disconnection from reality

Trying to lose inhibitions

Patterns of self-sabotage

Temporary fulfillment

Wanting excitement

Wanting peace

Illusions of instant enlightenment

Wanting connection

Alienation or loneliness

Curiosity

Experimentation

Avoiding creative fear

Managing emotions

Discomfort with success

When facing any of the above reasons for creating an addiction, try experimenting with the **Foundation Skills** and the **Tools for the Artist** in **Part III** before turning to sabotaging behavior. There are far better ways of addressing creative difficulties that can actually *increase* your artistic ability, and provide more access to your inner creative genius. Most writers have heard Hemmingway's cliché, "Write while drunk, edit while sober." We *are* more creative when free of the troubles, assumptions, or limitations of the mind, but there are healthier and more permanent ways of bypassing mental clutter than creating a sabotaging habit.

FINDING OR OFFERING HELP WHEN NEEDED

If you are experiencing an unhealthy habit or substance abuse, please find effective and qualified help today. If someone close to you is burdened by an addiction, then do what you can to help them. Having compassion and becoming an "enabler" are not the same thing. Life can be difficult, and one of the worse things we can do is to withhold our help or kindness from someone who has fallen into an addiction. There are far better ways to deal with life's challenges than the illusions offered by an addiction - but *hearing this* - and *knowing it* - are two different things. It is said that one cannot find a solution with the same state of mind that created the problem. Because substance abuse hijacks how the brain works, seriously addicted people usually need qualified help to overcome the control of the addiction, and stand on their own two feet again.

The *Checklist of Possible Addictions and Sabotaging Habits* at the end of this chapter is not presented as a moral judgement on anything that a creative person has experienced. It is not meant to be a list of right-or-wrong, good-or-bad, or moral-or-immoral. It is a list of possible forces that can misdirect, disempower, or sabotage an artist or their creative work. The list is presented to help artists to reclaim their creative power, and redirect it with greater mastery, originality, and authenticity.

Please see the list of helpful organizations and resources in the Reference Section.

"From this hour I ordain myself loos'd of limits and imaginary lines.

Going where I list, my own master, total and absolute…

Gently, but with undeniable will,

Divesting myself of the holds that would hold me."

American writer and poet, Walt Whitman, *Leaves of Grass*, 1855

A CHECKLIST FOR POSSIBLE ADDICTIONS OR SABOTAGING HABITS:

Food

Sugar

Drugs

Alcohol

Nicotine

Control

Careless sex

Negative thinking

Comfort

Pain

Media, news, television

Pornography

Heartache

Shopping

Stimulation

Games

A need for approval

Mentally created scenarios

Emotional highs or lows

Addiction to fear or suspense

Addiction to a person or feeling

Self judgement

Self-persecution

Drama

Dishonesty

Risk

Violence

Adrenaline

Gambling

Attention

Being a victim

Looking for excitement

NOTES

"The Great Wave Off Kanagawa" (detail) 1849, by Japanese artist, Katsushika Hokusai. Color woodblock print, Number 21 in the series, Thirty-Six Views of Mount Fuji.

12

THE SEA OF TRANSITION

Artists who are evolving into their unique version of artistic mastery will occasionally find themselves in an uncomfortable place that I call the *Sea of Transition*. This transitional period can feel like being lost at sea - but in fact, it acts as a kind of "bridge" between one creative reality and another. It might also seem like a "void" or a period of "nothingness." But, the *Sea of Transition* is more like a temporary experience that creators might go through as a result of personal growth, transformation, or the birthing of a new level of artistic ability.

Sometimes, the *birthing of something new* requires that we separate from our old way of seeing or working in order to create work that is beyond what we can currently imagine. Teenagers often go through a period of rebellion as a transition between childhood and adult life. Caterpillars spend time as cocoons before becoming butterflies. The Sea of Transition can act as a similar state of change, preparing the artist to transform from one level of creative ability to the next.

If we are not aware that we are in such a period of transition, we might feel very lost and uncomfortable - with no direction or points of reference. Such periods are often misunderstood as depression, discouragement, artist's block, or even a "dark night of the soul." The change might actually be the Sea of Transition, and not a bad place to be in once we find a way to use to use the experience to our advantage.

The transition from one level of artistic ability to a higher level of creativity rarely happens overnight. When crossing The Sea of Transition, it is as if the artist's feeling of "nothingness" helps them to *let go* of the old way of creating - even if it was good work - before growing into their new ability. When an artist's old familiar creative drive suddenly disappears, it is easy to think that something is very, very wrong. But the artist can actually make very good use of their time in this transition period, and strengthen their skills for the unknown work to come.

TRANSITION PROJECTS

A helpful thing to do when in the "void," or the Sea of Transition, is to assign yourself a "Transition Project." As we always have creative energy with us, it must be used for something so that it does not "back up" and manifest as things we may not want. Having a good challenging Transition Project can keep us growing as artists, keep our minds sharp, teach us new things, and prepare us for the Inspired creative projects to come. Depending on the length of your period of transition, or "dry spell," a good Transition Project could be a new class, research, helping someone in need, travel to foreign lands, or a series of new work that stretches your creative skills.

When we are busy creating our best work, or deeply involved in an Inspired creative project, we rarely take the time to clean, organize, travel, maintain friendships, or explore new territory. But in between periods of creative clarity and Inspiration we can use our time to grow in areas that might be neglected during long hours in the studio.

So many brilliant and talented artists have had a difficult time in the Sea of Transition, because they don't realize that is a normal part of growth as an artist. It can feel tragic and painful to fear that you have lost the artistic direction that once brought so much joy. It can be difficult to accept that the one thing that you could depend on is no longer true for you. Some might even fear a loss of identity. Extreme discomfort with the Sea of Transition might tempt some artists to fall into substance abuse in an attempt to feel something other than a scary emptiness. Some may use the discomfort of "not knowing what to do" as an excuse to get high, scatter their creative energy, or abandon their art form.

But *understanding* and *accepting* the purpose of being in the Sea of Transition can help the artist to make good use of it. Assigning yourself a

Transition Project that is fun, expansive, challenging, and good for you can contribute to artistic mastery.

Sometimes, an artist's *lost* or *blocked* feeling *is* caused by some kind of Creative Obstacle that can be transformed. How can we tell the difference between the Sea of Transition and the challenge presented by an actual Creative Obstacle? When in a transitional period, the artist might feel like they are somehow becoming a different person. They may feel motivated to explore or learn something new. If you take steps to resolve a Creative Obstacle - like using the Tools for the Artist exercises in Part III - and *still* find yourself completely unmotivated to create in the familiar way, you may be in the Sea of Transition.

The inner Master Artist *likes* a challenge. It can't be forced, manipulated, or outsmarted. Usually, taking the time to travel, learning new skills, or taking on some challenging work that is *beyond* your comfort zone, will open the door to more Inspiration and enthusiasm.

Losing interest in your work may be a sign that a period of transition is approaching, meaning that it's time to grow as an artist - both inwardly and outwardly. It is easy to lose interest in our work when we are not creating at our true level of ability, according to how our inner Master Artist wants to create. The mind may be satisfied and happy that we are busy and getting work done. But our inner Master Artist can become bored with mere busy work, or work that is not Inspired, or does not stretch or challenge our abilities. It typically wants to feel alive, to evolve, to be authentic, and to take creative risks. It is curious, visionary, and eager to learn. Can you imagine artists like Puccini or Mozart being willing to create *below* their ability level? Would Ansel Adams be happy with staying home to watch TV on the couch? Could Benjamin Franklin settle for being just a regular guy?

If you have lost motivation in the middle of a creative project, it helps to start asking yourself questions… A good one is, "If I were twice the Master Artist that I am now, what would this work look like? Another is, "If anything were possible, what would I do now?" Or, "Ten years from now, what am I going to wish I had done?" Often, asking such a question is enough to see more clearly, regain your enthusiasm, and get excited about the working again. Sometimes, the smallest of changes can make a difference and bring back the artist's enthusiasm. And sometimes the answer is not what we want to hear, like: "Wipe it down and start over." Or "This just isn't true for me anymore...." Regardless of how inconvenient it is to sacrifice work that represents an investment of time and materials, the freedom to create more powerful, original, and engaging work can be priceless.

3 THINGS TO REMEMBER ABOUT TRANSITION PERIODS

- The transition between one level of artistic ability and the next level rarely happens overnight - there is often a blank space, or void, between the two realities.

- A period of transition can be used to the artist's advantage by taking time to learn, travel, explore, and grow as an artist.

- Our inner Master Artist is always growing, moving, and evolving, so we must be growing, moving, and evolving to keep up with it.

Whether a journey through the Sea of Transition is a matter of days, weeks, or even months, it can be an empowering time for the artist if used wisely. Map out a transition show of work. Get healthier. Get better organized. Have adventures. Explore what you love. Learn something new. Keep your brain sharp. Expand your awareness. Volunteer to help someone. Go to the opera. Practice your skills. Get better acquainted with your True Self. Do things that make you a better person and a better artist - when inspiration presents itself, you'll be in the best shape to meet the challenge.

> "It looks sad and terrible before the crossover move that lets the nine levels of ascension turn into ordinary ground." Rumi

CHECKLIST OF HELPFUL ACTIONS WHEN CROSSING THE SEA OF TRANSITION:

Travel and Adventure

Volunteering

Help someone in need

Running, dancing, biking, or hiking

Time in nature or wilderness

Strengthen your skills

Beautify your environment

Explore other art forms

Painting, writing, sculpting

Regular meditation

Assign yourself a Transition Project

Time with loved ones

Questioning for Clarity exercise

Attend live music or theater

Get stronger and healthier

Get rid of old clutter or unused things

Writing short stories

Painting live landscapes or models

Create a better studio

"Boreas" 1903, by English painter, John William Waterhouse. Oil on canvas 32" x 25" Private collection.

13

SELF DOUBT AS AN ARTISTIC CHALLENGE

Every artist and creative person faces Self Doubt from time to time. So, if you are now experiencing doubt about your creative work, or about yourself as an artist, don't take it so personally. You're in good company. When we face a period of Self Doubt that actually interferes with our ability to do our best work, we can transform that doubt into a greater level of creative confidence. Self Doubt can also be like a "guardian at the door" of our next level of artistic ability, making sure that we are ready and willing to do our best work.

Self Doubt is a Creative Obstacle that almost every creative person will experience at some time. This is normal. When it is time to grow as an artist, we enter unfamiliar creative territory, where it becomes easy to doubt ourselves and our creative work. Self Doubt can look like feelings of inadequacy, unworthiness, insecurity, indecision, or discouragement. We may believe that we are untalented, uninteresting, or unqualified to be creative. We may become unsure of what we want to say, because we are not sure of *who we are* in this new territory. When your inner artist decides that it's time to grow, but we resist our own evolution, Self Doubt might be a friend giving you a kick in the pants.

When an artist falls into a pit of Self Doubt that is so encompassing that it interferes with their creative work, it rarely helps to hear prefabricated slogans like "Believe in yourself," or "Be positive." Obviously, if we could just "snap out of it," we would have already done so. In such situations, we can find the *cause* or *reason* behind the doubt so that we can reclaim our trapped creative energy. Are we doubtful because we know we can do better? Are we doubtful because of something unkind said to us? Are we doubtful because of past experiences? Are we taking other's opinions or actions too personally? Are we being as authentic as we could be? There are so many possibilities… But regardless of the reason, all sources of creative doubt can be transcended or transformed into better art. Self Doubt, or doubt about the creative work that we are doing, can be seen as a "bundle of energy." We can reclaim that energy once we address the inner reasons for our doubt and transform them.

Doubt can be your friend. There are times when we *should* question our own motives, methods, or intentions as artists. In order to become more authentic and more masterful in our creative work, Self Doubt can inspire us to pursue a higher perspective and a deeper meaning. Often, when we doubt it is because we want to know *the real truth* of something beyond what is currently apparent. If you are creating below your true ability level, doubt about your work might be saying that it's time to grow.

Sometimes, the Self Doubt is well founded. If we start to build a house, but have no building experience, doubt may be telling us to find some more experienced help. We may need to expand our skills and study plumbing, electrical systems, or woodworking. We may want to go one step at a time to make sure the foundations are lasting. We may want to study the soil quality and consider the light exposure. If you *support your inner creator* by learning everything that you need to know, confidence will build naturally.

Another form of Self Doubt is a sense of "lack." Feelings of *lack* sound like "I am not enough," or "I don't have enough…" or, "There isn't enough…" Sometimes, we place these judgements against ourselves based on life experience, or perhaps comparing ourselves to other artists. And sometimes, these ideas are planted in our heads by parents, society, or other influential people in our lives. If this is the case, The Art of Forgiveness might be your first stop in the Tools for the Artist section. All sources that played a part in creating a sense of lack can be thoroughly forgiven in order to fully let go of such limiting beliefs. The Tools for the Artist and the Foundation Skills in Part III will be useful for developing a greater sense of confidence, determination, self respect, and a strong foundation.

Situations that can leave us vulnerable to creative doubt are things like self judgement, taking things personally, being dishonest with our self, being less than authentic, avoiding challenges, creating to impress other people, creating work that is meaningless to us, pretending to be something we are not, withholding something important, exposure to sabotaging people, postponing self-care, refusing to evolve, and other disempowering choices.

Situations that can help to avoid creative doubt are things like generosity, love and kindness, doing work we really love, forgiving past failures or disappointments, being our True Self, taking good care of the artist, meditation and inner work, having a sense of humor, regular fun exercise, learning what you need to know, growing and improving as an artist, time with good friends, and other empowering choices.

DOUBT BASED ON PAST FAILURES

Creative Self Doubt can also develop as a result of guilt, shame, or past mistakes. If an artist has betrayed their self, or let their self down in some way, they may feel unable to have self-trust or self-confidence. Maybe they have caused harm, broken promises, or deceived others in the past. They may have experienced a big failure and were blamed harshly. Such memories can distill into general Self Doubt that can affect an artist's creative work. But it's usually not our mistakes and failure, but our *self judgement* about those mistakes and failures, that turns into creative Self Doubt.

For example, an aspiring fashion designer might be ready and motivated to create a whole new line of clothing - only to have the voices of Self Doubt creep in saying, "Sure, you'll let yourself and everyone down, just like before - you'll always be a loser." It's hard to maintain confidence in the face of such self judgement. HEY, EVERYONE MAKES MISTAKES! EVERYONE HAS FAILURES! No one is special in that department. Everything we learn from past mistakes, failures, and disappointments can make our creative work even more powerful, brilliant, and original.

There are steps that you can take if your Self Doubt is based on past mistakes or failures: **Step one** is to *forgive yourself* for any mistakes or failures - especially any related self judgement. Keep forgiving yourself as often as it takes. (see the Art of Forgiveness in Part III) **Step two** is to correct any doubt-producing mistakes that are possible to fix. Apologize to anyone harmed by those mistakes (including yourself), if it helps to resolve the issue. For those who are no longer around, you can always write a letter, and then burn it to Let Go of the energy. **Step three** is to make an action plan for your creative project to help you stay on track when doubt reappears. Create a good Guiding Star. (page 169) Any Self Doubt that was created by past mistakes can be transformed into creative confidence when we use what we have learned from those experiences to become a stronger person, and a better creator. **Step Four** is giving yourself "credit" for everything that you have learned from past mistakes or failures, just like the class credit one gets in art school or college.

3 THINGS TO REMEMBER ABOUT SELF DOUBT

- All artists and creative people experience Self Doubt, as it is a normal part of the growing process.

- Creative Self Doubt can be a friend that encourages you to do your best, most meaningful, and most authentic work.

- All doubt about your creative work can be seen as a bundle of energy that can be transformed into new levels of creative ability.

Creating a good Guiding Star (page 169) can keep you motivated and Inspired in challenging times. If judgements or projections coming from other people are undermining your creative confidence, take steps to protect yourself from such negative influences, both physically and psychically. Keep using the Skills and Tools in Part III to transform periods of Self Doubt into your next level of artistic mastery.

My Dragon of Self Doubt is dark, heavy, and oppressive. It's hard to breath when he is sitting on top of me. He reminds me of my failures and shortcomings, creating a sense of worthlessness. The Dragon might mention how great, talented, smart, and sophisticated other artists are, and that I've gained five pounds in the last month. The first thing I need to do is move - to go for a run and shake off the feeling of oppression. I might examine my current creative project to make sure that it is as true, authentic, and dynamic as I would want it to be. I thoroughly forgive the thoughts that created the Doubt Dragon, and made him so powerful. I then send him love, compassion, and understanding until we both start to laugh, and I regain my determination, optimism, and sense of humor.

"If you hear a voice within you saying, "You are not a painter," then be all means paint, boy, and that voice will be silenced, but only by working."

Dutch painter, Vincent Van Gogh in a letter to his brother, 1883

CHECKLIST FOR THE VOICES AND SIGNS OF CREATIVE SELF DOUBT:

I am not qualified

I am not worthy

I am not good enough

No one will listen to me

I am not entitled

I let people down

Trying to copy another's work

Withholding something important

I don't deserve to create something great

Creating an addiction is easier

I am inadequate as an artist or creator

Busy work as avoidance

They will never love or respect me

Discouragement

God doesn't care for me

Feeling hopeless

No matter what I do, I will fail

I have nothing original to say

Why should I bother

I don't have enough skill

I have no right to want to be better than I am

Lack of determination

Feelings of shame or guilt

Lack of confidence

Inferior/superior complex

In a transition period

Associating with unkind people

I must be crazy

There is no room for me

Comparing to other artists

I'm boring

NOTES

"The Loge" c.1878, by American painter, Mary Cassatt. Oil on canvas 31" x 25" National Gallery of Art, Washington, D. C.

14

LIMITING BELIEFS THAT HIDE YOUR ARTISTIC GENIUS

When a creative person wants to access their inner genius and Inspiration, it might help to let go of a few Limiting Beliefs. The Master Artist Within defines a Limiting Belief as an assumption or superstition that the artist has accepted as truth, that is *not necessarily true*. Belief is *thinking* that something is true, rather that *knowing* it. Such sabotaging beliefs could sound like: "The professor said that good art must follow certain rules." "I can only be a good artist if I get into a particular school," or "Great ballerinas must look a certain way." Limiting Beliefs can also include self-created superstitions like "I'm too old to start writing plays," or "I'll be a bad parent if I focus on my pottery before the kids grow up."

Where do such Limiting Beliefs come from? From family, art critics, institutions, society, advertising, cultural brainwashing, misinformed instructors, childhood conditioning, and the world in general. Many people and institutions actually communicate Limiting Beliefs in order to promote their own agenda and maintain some kind of dominance in their field. We might also create our own Limiting Beliefs after difficult life experiences: "If I stay away from painting elephants, I won't be rejected from another art show." Or, "If I get plastic surgery, I'll be a better actor." Or," I'll be safe as long as I pretend to be somebody else." When we transcend and let go of such beliefs, we free ourselves to create more authentically.

HIDDEN BELIEFS

Some Limiting Beliefs, especially the ones from media or childhood, may be so *ingrained* in our subconscious mind that their presence is only known by our actions, our fears, and how we create. How do artists forgive, overcome, or transform a sabotaging belief that we can't even identify? We start by doing what we can to re-educate our subconscious parts by doing challenging work that is outside of our "comfort zone." Tools for the Artist in Part III, like Writing for Clarity, can also help to awaken creativity hidden by Limiting Beliefs. Creating a Guiding Star that reminds us of our artistic intention can help to "re-educate" our mysterious hidden belief systems. Actions speak louder than words. So, the more we create challenging and authentic work that we love, the more our inner limitations can transform into confidence.

GIVE YOURSELF CREDIT

Limiting Beliefs can also develop when we use difficult life experiences *against* ourselves, rather than to our advantage. Everyone experiences failure, rejection, and disappointment. Many judges, critics, or art world people have their own issues. And we can judge our own work pretty harshly at times. Being a very creative person, I have made a shocking number of mistakes in my life. And, I've lived through my share of rejection, failure, disappointment, betrayal, embarrassment, and other heartaches. Oddly, all such experiences tend to produce stronger creative work once we empower ourselves by forgiving the judgements and attachments connected to them.

In order to make the *best use* of life's disappointments, we can learn to "give ourselves credit" for all of those rotten experiences. Just like the classes that we attend in art school or university, we can assign ourselves "points" or "class credit" for all the lessons learned in the school of life. "Four units for ruining a good painting... six units for stowing away on that ship to the Canary Islands... ten units for a broken heart…" After my many mistakes and challenges as an artist, I have accumulated quite enough "class credit" to create a methodology for transforming Creative

Obstacles, thank you. If you ever feel burdened by Limiting Beliefs created in the crucible of past experiences, then by all means, start giving yourself long overdue *credit* for what you have survived, what you have learned, and what you have mastered. Whether you use gold stars, a wreath of laurel leaves, or a fancy document written in calligraphy - claim all of life's experiences as an important part of your road to Creative or Artistic Mastery.

Whenever you hear yourself saying or thinking, "That brilliant idea isn't possible because___," challenge that belief. I'll tell you a secret: Most Limiting Beliefs are backed up by reasoning, theory, proof, and justification. Your inner creative genius, on the other hand, *needs no justification to exist.* Your inner Master Artist, like love, is its *own reason* for existing, can stand on its own, and is its own authority.

Our inner Master Artist, the source of creative genius inside of us, is no respecter of Limiting Beliefs - regardless of where those beliefs came from. We might believe that we are not capable of producing a masterpiece, but our inner Master Artist is not limited by such beliefs. If you have an undeniable inspiration to write an opera, but your Limiting Beliefs remind you that you aren't qualified - just start writing. Take a class. Spend time in Vienna. Limiting beliefs and superstitions can be challenged by "starting where you are," one small step at a time.

3 THINGS TO REMEMBER ABOUT LIMITING BELIEFS

- Limiting beliefs and superstitions are temporary illusions that can interfere with the our creative mastery and authinticity.

- Most works of creative mastery were made by artists who transcended custom, superstition, and limiting beliefs.

- Challenging, questioning, and transforming a false belief can open a new world of creative possibilities.

Sometimes, we might believe that we must know the outcome before starting a creation. When reaching into your inner *Unknown World* to create something new, the question of "how to take the next step" will usually not become clear until *after* we take the first step. How can you possibly know what is next, or how the next problem will be solved, if you are creating something that has never existed before? Many great creations have started as a note on a paper napkin, or a scribble in a sketchbook. If you have love, inspiration, and true enthusiasm for your vision, just start where you are.

Most false assumptions and Limiting Beliefs that block creativity cannot stand up to intelligent questioning - which is exactly why oppressive governments or religious orders have historically not allowed such questioning. Questions such as "How can the world be flat? Where is that chariot carrying the sun across the sky? Why shouldn't a woman paint as well as a man? Why should we care more about one child than another? There was a time when this type of questioning could get one into big trouble. Once you identify your beliefs about what is and is not possible as an artist, you can begin with the questions in Ch. 28, Questioning for Clarity, to see if those beliefs serve you or block you.

My Dragon of Limiting Beliefs is like a ghost in that he is almost invisible. I am often not even sure if he is there or not. He is full of proof and evidence why he is right, and why I am not qualified to create what I want. He tells me that I need to control or manipulate a situation because I have no other option. He makes me feel like I am a less powerful, less entitled, and less resourceful creator than I really am. When he shows up in the middle of a creative project - I realize that it is because a belief has put limitations on what I *think* is possible. But I can pull out my sword of Light and Love, and observe the Dragon for the illusion that he is. As I become more honest with myself about what it is that I *really* want to create, the building enthusiasm transforms the Dragon into more energy and excitement - often with unexpected help showing up out of nowhere.

> "How he comes o'er us with our wilder days, not knowing the use we made of them."
>
> Henry V 1:2, William Shakespeare

CHECKLIST FOR LIMITING BELIEFS ABOUT CREATIVITY AND THEIR SOURCES:

Childhood experiences

Parents or authority figures

Social programming

Entertainment and media

Art school

Rejections or failures

Who is or is not worthy

I must suffer to create

Artists look a certain way

It's hopeless to try

There are rules about…

I don't look or sound like…

I can't start until…

God will punish me if…

Sinners aren't entitled to…

I am not good enough

I am not qualified

I'm not contemporary enough

I don't belong

I was born into the wrong family

Cultural or racial roles

Astrological information

All master artists are dead

Feeling inferior or superior

My karma is holding me back…

Art is a waste of time

I need to be high to create

I am only a product of my environment

There aren't enough resources

Everything good has already been created

I am not smart enough

I have nothing worthwhile to say

Art must be shocking to be original

Good art is supposed to look a certain way

There are too many obstacles to overcome

NOTES

"Carolina Parakeets" (detail) 1885, by John James Audubon. Watercolor, graphite, pastel, gouache, and ink on mounted paper. These birds, native to the U.S., are now extinct. The New York Historical Society.

15

CREATIVE SABOTAGE

In the Master Artist Within manual, Creative Sabotage is defined as anything that we do, or anything that another might do, to block or undermine our creative work. Sabotage is a method of *withholding* or *blocking* our creative vision, and the gifts we might have to share with the world. Whether the sabotage comes from inside of the artist, or from an outside source, all Master Artists have had to deal with Creative Sabotage at one time or another.

How could another person or group sabotage an artist's creative work? Here are a few examples:

- Saying or writing hurtful or negative things about the artist
- Misrepresenting the artist to suit some agenda
- Purposely creating disturbances in the artist's studio
- Doing things to undermine the artist's confidence or peace of mind
- Envy, greed, or resentment as motivation to undermine the artist
- Creating unnecessary drama to get attention from the artist
- Actions meant to interfere with the artist's creative process.

People have all kinds of reasons for being small, petty, greedy, envious, prejudiced, needy, or just plain old mean. We don't have to figure out their motives or blame anyone. Creative people do, however, need to take the necessary steps to protect their work, environment, and well-being.

If you are an artist who is experiencing some sort of Creative Sabotage coming from the "outside world", it becomes *your* responsibility to protect yourself and your creative work. It is *your* responsibility to make yourself resilient in the face of negativity, and to maintain proper boundaries where needed. Part of artistic mastery is creating at your very best in any situation - even if that means creating a new studio or work space. Remember that any creative challenge, including sabotage, can be transcended or transformed to benefit the artist.

An artist can create protection from outside interference in several ways. The most obvious way is to remove yourself from a place where sabotaging forces can have access to you and your creative work. If the sabotage is coming from a loved one, we must be clear about our boundaries when doing creative work. If our work as an artist is important to us, we need to learn how to maintain healthy boundaries. One of the Foundation Skills is to create an Artist's Studio that is free from disturbance. You need to focus on the voice of your own inner Master Artist while creating, rather than the influence of other people.

Perhaps the most effective protection is to be connected to your True Self, to maintain a sense of humor, and learn to love unconditionally. In such a state of being, unkind things said or done by other people can become irrelevant.

To create authentically, it helps to make ourselves as "bullet proof" as possible in the face of critics or judgmental people. The more we let go of tendencies to worship the opinions of others, and our own temptations to judge others, the more resilient we become when faced with negativity. The more we create as our True Self, the less vulnerable we are to what others say or do. The more enthusiasm we have for our work, the less we care what others think.

Artists and creative people may also may need to *energetically* protect themselves at times. The world is full of psychic energy, radio waves, global disturbances, and other influences that might affect a sensitive artist. Some creative people are particularly perceptive and sensitive to other people's energies. This is great when there is a lot of love and goodwill in the air. But not so great when we have negative energy being directed toward us and our work. A good reason to expand our capacity to love unconditionally, is that we become more energetically protected when love is radiating *out* from us. Unconditional love has a transmuting effect on whatever is in its presence. The protection provided by *absolute love* is one of those things that can sound unbelievable if one has never experienced the phenomenon, but I highly recommend experimenting with it. It also helps to imagine light around the torso and creative section of the body - the area of the second chakra, between one's navel and knees.

SELF SABOTAGE

Some artists have a tendency to sabotage their own work for a variety of reasons. Perhaps they fear sharing their work with the world, perhaps it is a form of self-punishment, or perhaps they are afraid of discovering their inner Master Artist. I have seen gifted students actually "dumb down" their creative genius in the presence of friends or family in order to avoid making others feel bad or jealous. Any Creative Obstacle in Part II can have a sabotaging effect on your creative work. But Creative Sabotage is when we either consciously, or unconsciously, try to keep our best creative work from happening, or do something to ruin it when it does happen.

An artist's tendency to continually sabotage their creative work is a way of "withholding" their creativity for some reason. To "withhold" creative energy is to try to keep creative expression from happening, or to avoid sharing it with the world. The tricky thing is that our creative energy *will* express itself - with or without our permission. Even deciding what to have for dinner is a creative act. If we are holding back our creative energy, that energy can run amuck and create things that we may not want. Drug dealers know this. Scam artists know this. Advertisers know this. There are businesses waiting to profit from unused and available creative energy. All that creative energy with nowhere to go can be seduced into all kinds of actions. When we are devoting our creative energy to meaningful creative work or projects, we become much less vulnerable to distractions and energy vampires.

Believe it or not, some creative people can become so attached to a "comfort zone" that they will actually block or sabotage their own creativity just to maintain the life to which they are accustomed. Even if very unhappy in their current situation, the possibility of change might be more frightening than a known, familiar, and predictable misery. Our inner Master Artist is anything but predictable. If you find that your creative projects or plans are constantly sabotaged or abandoned, ask yourself if there is a fear or an attachment that needs to be addressed.

Another type of inner Creative Sabotage happens when an artist uses ordinary life experience *against* their self or their work. Things that are said can be twisted into a negative meaning. The actions of others can be interpreted as an insult. Memory and history can be used as evidence that life is hopeless. Comments can be twisted into accusations. And a lack of sales can be used as proof that our art is a waste of time. A habit of taking everything in life as some kind of "evidence" against yourself or your work is definitely Creative Sabotage. Can you imagine how much creative energy it takes to constantly twist everything into a negative meaning? Enough to create amazing things once the energy is reclaimed and redirected. Such patterns can be challenged and transformed using the exercises in Part III. It's good to develop a habit of giving yourself *credit* and *respect* for your life experience. The inner Master Artist uses all life experience in a way that fuels, strengthens, and contributes to creative mastery.

Occasionally, a creative person will *withhold or deny* their Inspiration for a variety of reasons. Perhaps a of fear of persecution. Perhaps self doubt. Perhaps discomfort with their own greatness. Perhaps a concern that others may use their work to create harm. As odd as this sounds, such concerns do exist. Throughout history, some have twisted laws, literature, or sacred writings in order to control and manipulate people. Tools that were designed to benefit mankind have been used for violence. Science, medicine, and psychology have been used both for and against people. Galileo was almost burned at the stake for trying to prove that the earth revolved around the sun, and not the other way around. But if we *withhold* the creations of our inner Master Artist out of fear, then the darkness wins. It has always taken great courage to birth a new creation into the world, not knowing what will happen.

If you have been experiencing Creative Sabotage from either the outside world or your own actions, the exercises in Part III can help to turn this around. Developing good Foundation Skills can help to resolve or prevent issues with sabotage coming from other people or groups. Every one of the Tools for the Artist can be very effective for transforming the causes or reasons for sabotaging actions coming from *within* the artist.

3 THINGS TO REMEMBER ABOUT CREATIVE SABOTAGE

- Creative self-sabotage can be transformed once the artist identifies the fear, cause, or reason for withholding their work.

- A strong inner life, and the cultivation of unconditional love, can go a long way to protect the artist from any ill intent from other people or groups.

- Withholding your creativity can allow creative energy to manifest in undesirable ways, like extra weight, negative thinking, and unhealthy habits.

I imagine the Creative Sabotage Dragon as a fierce looking beast who is really afraid on the inside. It has cold eyes, poisonous claws, and sharp multi-colored scales protecting a soft and vulnerable interior. It sneaks in and wreaks havoc when no one is watching. But the Creative Sabotage Dragon can be transformed into a loyal ally, giving its creative energy back to the artist once it is brought out into the light. The Foundation Skills and the Tools for the Artist in Part III can provide protection for the creative person, transforming patterns of self-sabotage into fierce creative determination and enthusiasm

"There is a vitality, a life force, or energy, a quickening that is translated through you into action, and because there is only one of you in all time, this expression is unique. And if you block it, it will never exist through any other medium and will be lost… Keep the channel open."

American dancer and choreographer, Martha Graham

CHECKLIST FOR CREATIVE SABOTAGE:

Fear of being seen, or known

Self-punishment

Withholding from the world

Fear of persecution

Fear of the unknown

Fear of out-shining another

Worship of opinions

Fearing what others think

Lack of self-worth

Fear of failure or rejection

The need to control

Fear of not being perfect

Self-judgment

Fear of being used or plagiarized

Busy work

Feeling unentitled or unqualified

Attachment to comfort

Fear of being exposed

Not wanting to outshine another

Unknown fears

Fear of change

Fear of success

Protecting an image

Fear of your own power or spirit

Fear of being judged or exiled

Twisting words and actions into insults

Creating addictions

Hurting yourself in some way

"Seein' Things At Night" (detail) 1903, Painting by American artist and illustrator, Maxfield Parrish. Oil on paper, 21" x 15" An illustration for *Poems of Childhood*, by Eugene Field, 1904, private collection

16

THE MANY FACES OF FEAR

Fear, of course, is a natural part of being in a human body. Artists, musicians, writers, performers, and other creative people have often experienced a *particular kind* of fear: Creative Fear. To create original work, we must put our inner selves out into the world for everyone to see, accept, reject, and to judge. If someone judges our work, it is like they are judging the very nature of who we are. Thus, it can take great courage, self-confidence, and determination to present new work into the world.

Creative and innovative people have historically been seen as odd, different, or eccentric. In centuries past, being seen as "different" from other people could get someone jailed, exiled, or even burned at the stake. Fear of persecution can be crippling, and we may still hold such ancient memories somewhere in the human consciousness. So, what can we do with this kind of Creative Fear when it stands in our way? Fear holds a tremendous amount of creative energy. And once we identify and *inwardly transform* that Creative Fear, we can redirect that power and energy into better and more authentic art.

Some artists can immediately transmute fear into excitement or action, and even claim to create their best work when pressured by a deadline. Fear can be our friend, acting as the voice of wisdom in dangerous situations. Fear might actually help when common sense fails us. It is when we allow creative fear to unnecessarily interfere with our art that it becomes a creative block or limitation. A fear of alligators might wisely block us from swimming alone in the Florida Everglades. But a fear of failure, a fear of being judged, a fear of rejection, or even a fear of the unknown, need not block us from doing our best creative work.

We may not always recognize our current creative challenge as some type of type of "fear." We may think that we are dealing with procrastination, an overwhelming schedule, a lack of the right conditions, or other excuses when avoiding our work - when in fact, there is an underlying fear that we are unwilling or unable to acknowledge.

For example, if we have a "fear of being ridiculed" for our writing, we might create a mountain of busy work just to avoid facing that fear. We might write about inconsequential things in an attempt to convince ourselves that we are doing good work. But once we identify, embrace, and transform the inner "fear of being ridiculed," we can reclaim our creative energy and use it to become an even better writer.

An artist may privately believe their talent to be inadequate, and fear discovering that they just might be right. Instead of taking a class or trying to transform the fear, they would rather create all kinds of problems that need "fixing" in order to avoid facing that fear. Serious addictions have been created in an attempt to avoid the fear of failure, the fear of inadequacy, and even the fear of becoming more powerful creators than we ever imagined. Needless to say, there are more empowering ways to address a Creative Fear than numbing or harming one's self.

Trying to avoid the feelings associated with our creative fear can turn into more serious problems. When we try to ignore, hide from, or overcompensate for our fears, they can easily turn into anxiety, or even full on panic attacks. Panic attacks are no fun, and many self-sabotaging decisions have been made in an attempt to make them go away - drinking, isolation, substance abuse, and hiding from the world. Such answers never work for long, and just disempower the artist.

Of course, it may sound like a ridiculous bumper sticker to hear someone say, "Embrace your fear" when the artist is having a full-blown panic attack. But in fact, learning to love, embrace, and have compassion for the fearful part of us is perhaps the best way to permanently transform such fear without the use of drugs. As impossible as this sounds, overcoming panic and anxiety is a skill that can be learned through meditation, writing, the Art of Forgiveness, and other ways of engaging hidden fears.

In his MC2 Method material, Reid Reichardt says that "Panic comes from extreme avoidance of feelings." I have found this to be true. After prayer, meditation, distraction, affirmations, hypnosis, herb tea, clearing techniques, and a lot of alcohol failed to get rid of my severe panic attacks, learning his refined method of transforming fear *finally* worked for me. (Please see the Reference Section) I was amazed by the creative energy that I was able to reclaim by becoming friends with my worst fears, rather than trying to disown them.

Everyone wants to avoid bad feelings. The problem is that we have a tremendous amount of creative energy stored up in those parts of our consciousness where the uncomfortable feelings are stored. Those uncomfortable feelings represent a part of us. So, if we want to *reclaim* all that energy and free it up for our creative work, we must make it feel welcome and listen to what is has to say. We learn to become more *comfortable* with our feelings Paradoxically, once we start to welcome the fearful parts of our inner world, they start to transform in surprising ways.

Paying attention to where you place your focus can also help to keep Creative Fear from developing. Another fear that has influenced my creative freedom is claustrophobia - an uncontrollable fear of being trapped. With a group of friends, I once walked through an underground aqueduct in Israel called Hezekiah's Tunnel, which runs under the old part of Jerusalem. We were in total darkness with water up to our chests, and far from any exit, when I started to seriously panic. I noticed that as I paid attention to my desire to escape, the claustrophobia grew worse. But, when I focused on sending love and light out to the people around me, to the tunnel, and to all of Jerusalem, the claustrophobia magically went away. Ever curious, I played with transferring my focus back and forth between possible escape routes and my caring for others. While standing in the water, I observed the panic come and go according to where I placed my energy. I was amazed by how the energy of fear could be transformed through the redirection of my focus and attitude.

FROM FEAR TO ENTHUSIASM

Love, compassion, and enthusiasm have transformative powers, and they become powerful allies in the presence of Creative Fear. We have the greatest enthusiasm for the art we most love, and most love to do. Thus, it becomes important to pay attention to what inspires our greatest enthusiasm, whether we understand it or not. The Greek source of the word *enthusiasm* is "God's energy, divine Inspiration, or God within." Enthusiasm generates its own energy and comes with its own genius. When we work in the area of our greatest enthusiasm, and when we truly *love* what we are creating, Creative Fear is replaced by excitement. The truth is - and every artist must find this out for themselves - we are much more creative and powerful that any fear or illusion that life can throw at us. Learning to master the *energy* tied up in creative fear is part of learning to create as a Master Artist.

3 THINGS TO REMEMBER ABOUT CREATIVE FEAR

- Our Creative Fears hold a lot of energy that can be transformed and redirected into greater artistic mastery and enthusiasm.

- As our Creative Fears represent a valuable part of our inner world, befriending our fear empowers us to become better artists.

- Many creative blocks, limitations, and other challenges can actually begin with some kind of underlying fear of what the artist is capable of creating or being.

When faced with a Creative Fear, experiment with the Tools for the Artist in Part III. Try to be optimistic even in the absence of reason. Be willing to take the next step in your creative work. Have faith. As we practice the transformation of each Creative Fear that presents itself, it becomes easier to have faith. With experience, faith eventually morphs into confidence, and eventually confidence can become mastery.

My Fear Dragon usually shows up in the region of my chest, sometimes extending into my stomach. Sometimes he has spikes like a porcupine, at other times he's dark and smoky like an electrical storm cloud. He is actually quite sensitive for such a threatening creature. The more I welcome him, talk to him, and listen to what he has to say, the more docile he becomes. The more kind and attentive I am towards him, the more he releases my creative energy back to me. The more active I am in my creative work, the more he seems to be on my side. It's OK when the Fear Dragon unexpectedly shows up for a surprise visit, because I now know that he's ultimately on my side. Often, just singing the right song or playing the right music is enough to relax him altogether.

> "Obstacle cannot crush me… Every obstacle yields to stern resolve. He who is fixed to a star does not change his mind."
>
> Artist, engineer, inventor Leonardo da Vinci

CHECKLIST FOR POSSIBLE CAUSES, REASONS, OR TYPES OF CREATIVE FEAR:

A fear of:

Failure

Success

Recognition

Exile

Rejection

Judgements

Ridicule

Persecution

Exposure

Embarrassment

Truth

Abandonment

Offending someone

Causing harm

Being used

Being ignored

Feeling inadequate

Feeling unprepared

Being trapped

Disappointing someone

Overshadowing someone

Being disloyal to a culture

Offending a Higher Power

Destroying an image

Wasting time or money

Being wrong

Making mistakes

Losing touch with reality

Being misunderstood

Being misrepresented

The Unknown World

Uncertainty or risk

Pain

Power

Authority figures

Not being as good as another

Hidden shame or secrets

Being disloyal to an image

One's own creative power

Being perceived as crazy

Poverty

"Starry Night" (detail) 1889 by Dutch painter, Vincent van Gogh. Oil on canvas, 29" x 36", painted during his time at an asylum near Saint-Remy-de-Provence in France. The Museum of Modern Art, New York, N.Y.

17

WHEN ARTISTS GO CRAZY

Historically, there have been many artists, innovators, and creative geniuses who have been labeled as crazy, insane, or in a world of their own. In this chapter, we will look at some of the reasons why an artist might occasionally feel Crazy, or at least perceived as Crazy. To be very clear, I am not a psychiatrist or psychologist - my doctorate degree is in theology. My observations about artists being labeled as "crazy" come from *being* an artist, counseling other artists, having artistic friends and students, having a creative family, and my obsession with art history.

Many artists and creative people have had periods of time when they felt *Crazy*, alienated, or doubted their perception of reality. The image of a "crazy artist" is such a cliché - an understandable cliché, as artists often do need to let go of "normal life" in order to bring original and innovative works of art into the world. There is often a lot of risk involved in creating new things, and risk can make one feel less than secure in life and in society.

Of course, sometimes *there is* an actual medical reason for feeling imbalanced. When physical or mental health is a factor, the creative person needs to find qualified help as soon as possible before getting back to their creative work. (Please see page 144)

Once an artist starts to pursue a greater level of creative ability, they often leave behind the familiar way of seeing things in order to expand into "unknown inner territory." Artists must let go of their preconceived notions if they want to create work that goes *beyond* preconceived notions. In order to visit a foreign country, we must leave the comforts of home for unfamiliar ground. In much the same way, creative genius and original ideas must come from beyond the *Known World*, beyond the usual reference points, beyond what the mind thinks, and beyond what friends might understand. So, if you are a creator producing miraculous works of art, of course some people might think you're Crazy, or at least a bit "different."

> "No excellent Soul is exempt from a mixture of madness."
>
> Aristotle, Greek philosopher and scientist, 384 BC-322 BC

Transition periods: Creating in the *Master Artist Zone* can be exhilarating - especially when creating with a new ability, genius, and energy coming from unknown heights that we did not know we had access to. After spending time in such a rarefied reality, where the artist might experience a "superhuman" self, it can be very difficult to return to the ordinary world, and an ordinary self. To return to normal life after such a period of creativity, the artist might feel lonely, lost, alienated, depressed, and sometimes separate from reality. Just like the culture shock that one experiences after living in a foreign country, or remembering how to walk on land after a journey at sea, the Master Artist must learn to comfortably traverse different realities if we want to create our best and most original work. Many artists are comfortable with the transition between the studio and the rest of the world, but some have a tougher time. It is helpful to be aware that creative people often *do* traverse different realities - and, we must learn to be comfortable with it, and even develop a sense of humor about it.

We can also feel Crazy when we are in a kind of void or transition period - sensing the urge to create, but not yet clear about what we *will* be creating. True artists are always growing - and when we grow or evolve into a new way of creating, we rarely just "snap into it." Usually, there is some time and space between our *old* way of being and the *new* way of creating. Sometimes the transitional period is only a few days, and sometimes it takes longer. Our inner Master Artist might know what is going on, but *we* usually don't. To create something original, we leave behind the security of everything that was created before. We might leave behind everything that gave us identity, value, security, recognition, and self-esteem. It takes great courage to risk going into new realms of creativity with no points of reference or guarantees.

Going through the emptiness that stands between how the artist *used to* create, and how the artist *will be* creating, can feel like being "lost at sea." (see The Sea of Transition, Ch 12) During these important periods, some creative people try to avoid the uncomfortable experience by drinking too much, self-medicating with drugs, or other sabotaging choices. It is vitally important to take good care of both your inner and your outer artist and avoid any self-damaging behavior. The Sea of Transition can produce valuable information, even when it feels like a "big dark nothing." This void can hold revelations that you might be needing when the Inspiration for a new project does appear. Make good use of the time between projects. Practicing, learning, hiking, traveling, exploring, writing, volunteering, doing anything for yourself or others will inwardly strengthen you for greater work, and help you to feel less Crazy.

Hopelessness: Of all the Crazy feelings creative people can face, one of the worst has to be a period of discouragement. Hopelessness, or discouragement, can feel impossible to resolve, because by its very nature, all possible solutions look "hopeless." Artists are *so* creative that they may have the ability to go deeper into despair than usual. It is important to recognize it for what it is - a temporary feeling. Sometimes, such feelings can be overcome with a hot shower, a good night's sleep, some high-quality exercise, or time with encouraging friends. But, sometimes more professional help is needed. Discouragement can come and go like a dark cloud, seemingly for no reason. If an artist has been working hard on a creative project, only to experience failure after failure, it becomes easy to slip into a deep hole of discouragement. The voice of Self Doubt might say things like, "My work is no good, why should I bother, I always fail, nothing will change, everything is a waste of time..." Never, never, ever let these voices win! Changes may be required, but never let *hopelessness* or *discouragement* have their way with you. If a consistent discouragement seems impossible to overcome, get help from a friend, a counselor, or a healthcare professional right away. (Please see page 144)

There are effective ways to transform the energy of hopelessness or discouragement into enthusiasm, confidence, and artistic mastery. Physical movement and exercise is important. Writing for Clarity, Sound and Frequency, and other Tools for the Artist in Part III, will help the artist to gain clarity, transform discouragement into enthusiasm, and take a new level of creative energy into the studio.

Different Realities: Another type of Crazy is when an artist loses their ability to discern what is, or is not, reality. The truth is, there *are* different levels and types of reality. Most artists have experienced dreaming while asleep at night, which is one example of a different reality where we regularly visit. We can also experience different inner worlds during meditation. When working on a big creative project, an artist may travel through different realms of imagination and different levels of consciousness in the course of creating something that has never before existed. They may emerge from the studio at the end of the day feeling like they have been "in a galaxy far, far away." When learning to create in the Master Artist zone, we must get used to creating in one world, and living with other human beings in this one. Even creative geniuses still have responsibilities in the physical world. Caring for our loved ones only contributes to our creative strength. Meditation is excellent for helping the artist to feel more comfortable with traveling between different realities.

Misdirected creative energy: Sometimes creative people can drive themselves crazy by creating a lot of unnecessary drama, negative thinking, or imagining things that are not really happening. Such things often happen when a highly creative person is *withholding* their creative energy, trying to create far below their ability level, or creating something that is in conflict with their true nature. Creative energy is very powerful, and when left unused, or misdirected, it can easily manifest as a feeling of craziness for the artist.

It's easy for very creative people to disperse their intense energy by over-creating in different ways. Spending too much money, trying to please too many people, agreeing to too many events, having too many parties, and starting too many projects are all examples of spreading one's attention too thinly. So much creative energy dispersed out into different directions can make it difficult to maintain the inner focus required for original and authentic work. Losing track of a sense of self by scattering one's focus can make an artist feel Crazy.

Anxiety: Periods of fear, anxiety, and panic attacks can also feel like another kind of Crazy. I know that when experiencing a full-on panic attack, with my body reacting in a way that I could not control, it felt like I was losing my grip on reality. Experiencing *fight or flight* reactions for no apparent reason – and, having a dose of adrenaline released into the body - can leave one feeling "separate from reality." This is not fun. If this happens, vigorous physical movement helps to use up excess energy and adrenaline. Singing helps to calm hyperventilation and regulate breathing.

Trying to avoid anxiety seems to only make it worse. Doing meditation to embrace the *source* of anxiety is an effective way to transform panic and anxiety without the use of drugs. The fear associated with anxiety represents a part of our inner world – when we stop, listen, and pay attention to the source of that fear, it can begin to transform. (Please see the Reference and Notes Section) When panic and anxiety are effectively transformed, there is often an increase of creative freedom, confidence, and enthusiasm.

Teenage years: Teenage artists often experience their own kind of feeling Crazy. Teenagers can be sensitive, and typically have a *tremendous* amount of creative energy. Thus, when they are not doing meaningful, exciting, and challenging work, all that creative energy can explode into all kinds of behavior: rebellion, anger, destruction, substance abuse, risky behavior, being unkind, negative thinking, weight gain, obsession with media, and other creations. But when given the chance, they are capable of producing amazing creative work that is often beyond what their teachers can do. During the teen years, when young people are so full of energy, it is crucial that they have access to instruction, guidance, and education that is meaningful, challenging, engaging, and motivating.

I first noticed the importance of "redirecting creative energy" when teaching high school students how to design and build stained glass windows. They had to learn how to handle hot soldering irons, dangerous chemicals, cut sheets of glass, and even become comfortable with the possibility of cutting or burning fingers in the process. There was something about the *challenge* of the art form that got their attention and respect. Eventually, I noticed that the most troubled and ill-behaved students often wound up creating the most impressive and original stained glass windows. All of that raging teenage creativity, when channeled into challenging work, produced a craftsmanship, originality, and artistry that made me envious. The students were *proud* of the difficulties that they had to overcome to produce such beautiful work. As dangerous as the art of stained glass can be, every semester there was still a waiting list to get into the class.

Physical well-being: Many creative people get so involved in their work that they forget to take the best care of themselves. Feeling mentally or emotionally "off balance" can be as simple as a health issue that is easily addressed. Physical exercise is needed to use up excess mental and emotional energy, and to maintain good circulation and brain function. Too much caffeine can contribute to anxiety and nervousness. Nutritionally, adequate vitamins, minerals, protein, and even water are important for feeling strong and resilient. Too much sugar can result in blood sugar issues that can have a big effect on one's state of mind. Drugs or too much alcohol will interfere with the artist's ability to think clearly and do their best work. Infections in the body can make a person feel odd, weak, or dizzy. Make sure that the air in the artist's environment is free from toxins. These are all common-sense things to consider if the artist is not feeling as mentally or emotionally well as usual.

3 THINGS TO REMEMBER ABOUT FEELING CRAZY

- Creative genius and original ideas often come from a reality other than ordinary life, and going there does not have to make the artist Crazy.

- Artists can to learn to gracefully transition between different realms of creativity while still maintaining their connection with friends, family, and a healthy life.

- If a creative person feels frightened about their state of mind, or is considering self-harm, they must immediately ask for help as their next act of creation.

Acts of kindness: Volunteering to help others - whether a neighbor, an animal shelter, or an organization - can also be very effective in turning around a confused or "crazy" state of mind. It may be hard to believe when in the midst of suffering through a dark or confusing time, but something *magical* happens when doing something kind to help another with love and compassion. Unconditional and selfless service is a beautiful act of creation. When performing an act of kindness, we get to experience a very powerful part of ourselves that is unaffected by life, our thoughts, our doubts, or the conditions of the world.

> "Shubert was crazy, you know. Do you think you have to be crazy to create something powerful?"

Spoken by the Josh character while listening to Ave Maria in a West Wing episode, 1999, written by Aaron Sorkin

    I imagine a variety of Crazy Dragons, depending on the situation, and try to maintain a sense of humor about all of them. We do have some interesting conversations, but it's hard to win an argument with one. The

Writing for Clarity exercise, followed by a good run, is usually my first choice for transforming an out of balance situation. It helps that I have spent enough time getting to know the nature of my True Self to be able to tell when I am "off-track." A talk with a good friend is also very helpful. Sometimes all that is needed is a different perspective - one of the benefits of cultivating strong friendships and a sense of humor.

HELP

Get help today if you need it! Being very powerful creators, some artists go so deeply into darkness that they cannot find a way out by themselves. You must resist all temptation to fall into destructive thinking or behavior when experiencing a period of feeling "crazy." So many creative people have fallen into the trap of self-destructive behavior during dark, hopeless, or uncomfortable periods. It is always a temporary state, even if it doesn't feel like it at the time. STAND YOUR GROUND, and make sure that you ask for the help you need. If you need medical attention for a condition, then by all means get that help immediately so that you can get back to doing your creative work.

If you feel hopeless, overwhelmed, or frightened by your state of mind, ask for help immediately!

Lifeline: 1-800-273-8255

suicidepreventionhotline.org

Panic attacks: selftherapy.org

 A local hospital emergency room

Also: friends, family, counselors, doctors, churches, fire stations, and local clinics.

"To anyone out there contemplating suicide remember this: some of your greatest revelations occur during the lowest points of your life. That rough road can still be navigated, so go on down it!"

Writer, traveler, and international big wave surfer, Jim Elder, 2017

CHECKLIST FOR ARTISTS FEELING CRAZY:

Thoughts of hurting yourself or others

Suicidal thoughts

Inability to care for yourself

Inability to function in the world

Need for certain nutrients

Being around unkind or toxic behavior

Exposing yourself to negative influences

Refusing to take care of yourself

Separating yourself from life

Feeling hopeless or discouraged

Uncontrollable panic attacks

Inability to complete work

Self-sabotaging behavior

Inability to trust anyone

Consistent depression

Imagining people are against you

Unfounded fear or paranoia

Creating overwhelm or confusion

Being dishonest with yourself

Substance abuse

Too much sugar, caffeine, or alcohol

Avoiding your work

Withholding your creative abilities

Withholding your creative genius

Withholding what is true for you

Withholding love or caring

Giving in to inertia or stagnation

Being overly sensitive

Insurmountable fear

Refusing to ask for help

Blood sugar issues

Infection in the body

Erratic emotions or moodiness

PART III

FOUNDATION SKILLS and TOOLS FOR THE ARTIST:

Transforming Creative Obstacles Into Artistic Mastery and Authenticity

"Mice Sewing the Mayor's Coat" (detail) c.1902, by English artist and illustrator, Beatrix Potter, illustration for the book, *The Tailor of Gloucester*. Watercolor on paper, Tate Gallery, London.

18

FOUNDATION SKILLS FOR MASTER ARTISTS

PART III begins with 10 important "Foundations Skills." These Foundation Skills are practices and techniques for daily life that are designed to encourage mastery, authenticity, and general well-being for creative people. Developing strong Foundation Skills can also help to protect the artist from unnecessary Creative Obstacles. Just like a castle overlooking a raging sea, creative people need a rock-solid foundation to do their best work, regardless of life's challenges. The following 10 Foundation Skills are designed to keep an artist strong, healthy, protected, and Inspired while growing into their next level of Artistic Mastery:

Skill #1. Take Excellent Care of The Artist

Skill #2. The Creative Power of Love and Kindness

Skill #3. Willingness

Skill #4. The Art of Paying Attention

Skill #5. The Importance of Movement

Skill #6. Practice Your Craft

Skill #7. Find Your Enthusiasm

Skill #8. A Healthy Sense of Humor

Skill #9. The Artist's Studio

Skill #10. Your Guiding Star

The time invested in creating a strong foundation is important to any creative project, and important to any artist. Anyone will find their creative focus "split" when overly concerned about health issues, mental sluggishness, outside interference, threats to their well-being, or an unsupportive environment. These Foundation Skills can help the artist to better prepare for new and surprising levels of creative ability. To create beyond your *current* ability, you may need to strengthen your body, improve your working environment, clear your mind of distractions, or make other changes to support yourself and your work in the studio. Most creative people today live in a complicated world with seemingly unlimited distractions, demands, and responsibilities. To create with a greater degree of mastery or authenticity, we need to develop the *inner strength* required to maintain our creative integrity in the face of such challenges. The following Foundation Skills can naturally improve inner strength, enthusiasm, creative ability, and even the ability to have more fun:

"I realized that in my time away, my brother had become an artist. He stood not on a riverbank, but suspended above the earth like a work of art, exempt from all its laws."

From the Robert Redford film, *A River Runs Through It,* 1992, based on a Norman Maclean story.

Skill #1: TAKE EXCELLENT CARE OF THE ARTIST

All art begins with the artist. Art begins *inside of the artist*. Improving artistic ability begins with improving something within the artist's inner world. In order to create your best, most Inspired, and most authentic work, taking good care of yourself on levels is a good place to start. You are the most important tool in the studio.

The need to "suffer for your art" is a myth. Creative people *do* tend to produce more Inspired and original work when they challenge themselves to create beyond their "comfort zone." But, it is important to take excellent care of ourselves while transcending our challenges.

Many big creative projects begin with a whole team of creators, producing a synergy that can result in art greater than the sum of individual efforts. From families to large companies, each team member can contribute their own part of the of magic if they have the care and support they need. Regardless of the source of Inspiration, our creative works are filtered through *our state of mind*, and the *state of our well-being*. Taking care of both the *inner* and the *outer* artist contributes to a sense of confidence, optimism, and self-esteem, which will show in in the quality of our work. One cannot fake creative mastery or Inspiration - it must come from the *inside* the creator.

Being well cared for can *prevent* many issues that interfere with creative work. As obvious as this sounds, if you are a busy, Inspired, and hard-working artist, it might be challenging to take the time needed to care for the very foundation of your creative work - your body, mind, and spirit. Believe it or not, taking care of yourself *as a creative priority* is one of the best things that you can do for your art.

Your brain, your heart, and all parts of your body depend on good nutrition, and good blood circulation to distribute oxygen and nutrients. The circulation of blood and oxygen can also clean your system of toxins and waste. Your body needs daily movement and exercise - preferably something fun and enjoyable - to keep your mind sharp and get your blood going in a lively way. Vigorous movement can also lift your spirits and make you less vulnerable to discouraging thoughts and feelings. Movement that enlivens both your body and state of mind, will have a positive effect on your creative work.

For an artist, your physical brain and mental well-being can translate Inspiration into the signals that enable you to create. So as artists, we are served by having a healthy brain. Your nervous system carries these signals to your hands, voice, feet, and body. Thus, your brain cells and nervous system need to be finely tuned and responsive to carry these messages from your inner genius to the parts of you doing the work. Given the importance of your brain and nervous system, nutrition, movement, fresh air, and high-quality sleep become your most important creative allies.

Your emotional well-being, or how you *feel* in the studio, also has an important influence on the quality of your work. Quality time spent with friends, family, loved ones, and other artists may seem like a distraction at times, but it actually contributes to our happiness and inner well-being. Again, our creative work begins *inside of us*, so it's important to make time for what makes you smile, laugh, and feel good inside. Whether it's volunteer work, time in nature, going on adventures, or seeing a live performance, we need things that lift our emotions and inspire a sense of wonder. We learn to not take things personally. We can cultivate emotional strength and a sense of well-being. Uplifting music matters. Friendships matter. Gratitude matters. Good art matters. A sense of humor matters. Clearing depressing things out of our environment can help. Most of all, cultivating a greater capacity to love matters to our creative work.

In addition to your creative work, it is important to pay attention to what you do with **your inner imagination**. In the privacy of your inner world, are you creating in a way that benefits your well-being, or do you imagine all kinds of discouraging or fearful scenarios? Our imagination can be like an inner studio, so be the master of your imagination. Imagine good things happening. Make sure that whatever you create in your imagination, that it supports you and your creative work.

How do artists take care of their spirit? This is a tricky question, as creative people have many different opinions about what spirit is, and what it means to be spiritually strong. When we create truly original and inspired work, we are reaching *beyond* our familiar world, and into an inner *Unknown World*. Through our art, we can bring the energy of that Unknown World into this world. This is why certain music, paintings, literature, and other creations seem to be so timeless and enduring generation after generation - their Inspiration came from a *different reality*. In the *Master Artist Within* material, we call this different reality "Spirit" as a way to describe the source of creativity that originates beyond our Known World.

Whether you see the source of your creative genius as God, the Universe, your Soul, a higher power, or your Muse, your *inner awareness* is your connection with that source. For some creative people, paying attention and focusing on the present moment is enough to stay spiritually connected. Others find it through an unconditional love, and sharing that love with the world. Many artists use prayer, meditation, and special rituals to keep themselves spiritually awake and connected. For artists, it's worth finding out what increases the Light and awareness of Spirit inside of you. It's worth discovering which practice helps you to transcend the already-created world in order to find the creative genius inside of you.

Your environment - where you live and work - can have a profound effect on how you create. This includes the physical space, the people around you, and even the sound that goes into your ears. The outer environment often winds up being a reflection of our inner environment. Mysteriously, clearing out or improving our work environment will have an uplifting effect on our inner environment. So, keep your environment healthy. Clear out or contain any solvents or toxins. Avoid unkind, distracting, or critical people when working. Be kind and encouraging towards others, and be of good cheer. Nurture your sense of humor. Create an uplifting vibe in your creative space that makes you happy just to walk in the door. Sounds and smells really matter. In the studio, trade in chaotic noise for silence, encouraging sound, or music that helps you to create in a happy and Inspired state of mind.

For most creative people, having to spend time on **money matters** can feel like a huge inconvenience. It seems that the part of the brain concerned with profit, and the artistic part, are like two different countries speaking different languages. Alas, such is the world we live in. Because Inspired creative people often live with one foot "in another world," artists throughout history have had money issues. The few artists who actually enjoy the business side of their art career seem have an advantage in the world. But, making sure that you and your family are well cared for is, in itself, a creative act. Even if the time spent on keeping your finances healthy seems like a big distraction, it is usually far more distracting and stressful to feel financially threatened. Respect yourself and your creative work enough to make sure that your inner artist is supported. Take excellent care of yourself.

If you find that you are having difficulty caring for yourself, your first step may be to ask for help. We are all designed to be connected to each other, and all need help at times. If you are currently experiencing serious difficulties like poverty, illness, abuse, addiction, or other challenges, your next important creative act must be to ask for help right away. Please see the Reference Section at the back of the book if you don't know where to start. Make your well-being more important than your circumstances. Getting the help that you need could be the most important next step on your journey to creative mastery.

"Self-love, my liege, is not so vile a sin as self-neglecting."

William Shakespeare, *Henry V*, 2:4

Skill #2: THE CREATIVE POWER OF LOVE AND KINDNESS

What do love, kindness, and compassion have to do with artistic mastery? How are qualities like creative genius, mastery, or authenticity related to love? It all has to do with the *frequency* and *state of mind* of the person creating. All art begins inside of the artist. When we are being compassionate, loving, or simply kind, we are being the best that a human can be. The heart and mind are more open, so the limitations associated with creative difficulties are not as present.

Negative feelings are burdensome. When you free yourself of judgments, worry, control, prejudice, and opinions, you become more available to your inner source of genius and Inspiration. When you love what you are creating, treat yourself with kindness, and cultivate acceptance towards others, you are actually creating a better world in addition to your art. In such a state of mind, we make ourselves available to a bigger world of artistic possibilities.

Through our thoughts and actions, we choose the level of energy that we want to work with. If in the private thoughts of our mind we are unkind to ourselves or others, then we are not in the frame of mind to create our best work. If we are using our valuable creative energy to manufacture negative thoughts and scenarios about ourselves or others, then that energy is not being directed by the inner Master Artist.

Caring for our family and loved ones, even though it seems unrelated to our creative work, actually builds up the energy of confidence and mastery in the artist - and it shows in the quality of our art. The love that we have for our family, friends, and animals all contribute to our inner mastery. Even though children may seem like a distraction, many artists find their creative ability and resourcefulness growing after becoming a parent. It's like babies are born with little crowbars in their fists that they use to pry our hearts open against our will - and that expanded capacity to love shows in our creative work.

I have lived long enough to learn that when I am riding on the energy of absolute love, I am creating at my best. Whether the love of nature, the love for our children, the love for a friend, the love for our art form, or even an expansive love for the whole universe - it is the most powerful state of mind for creating. Creative people know that when they truly love their work, a superhuman enthusiasm often seems to override tiredness or physical concerns.

What if a mindset of love, kindness, or compassion does not come easily? What if one's life experience has made it difficult to even relate to such feelings? Attitudes such as love, or kindness do not have to occur to us naturally - these are qualities that we can learn to cultivate. I was pretty indifferent to the whole human race until I became a mother - and started to see the original innocence hidden in everyone. The Tools for the Artist in PART III can be a good place to start for expanding one's capacity for love or compassion.

Anyone can start small - pay attention to the love of a song, the love for a work of art, a puppy that melts your heart - and practice expanding those feelings to other areas of life. Kindness can be practiced with just a smile or a nod to someone - even when you don't feel like it. Record in your Secret Journal little things that you appreciate about the world around you, regardless how insignificant. The more you pay attention to what you appreciate, the more the inner "radio dial" picks up on what touches your heart, cultivating compassion little by little. Once the heart starts to awaken, it shows in the quality of your artwork. Why should an artist bother to expand their capacity for love and kindness? Because love is the biggest creative power, and it empowers you as a creator.

Wouldn't love or kindness leave one's heart open to things like disappointment, hurt feelings, and broken hearts? Well of course, especially if we put rules, agendas, or conditions on our love, generosity, or compassion. The more *unconditional* we are in our love and kindness, the more we are protected. Absolute love has the ability to transmute negativity. Unconditional love is transcendence made manifest. A loving heart has the creative power to transmute everything into greater love, and greater artistic ability.

"Love many things, for therein lies the true strength, and whosoever loves much performs much, and can accomplish much, and what is done in love is done well."

Dutch painter, Vincent Van Gogh

Skill #3. WILLINGNESS

Willingness is such a simple word. Our decision to be *willing* or *not willing* to overcome Creative Obstacles can make a world of difference when it comes to increasing artistic mastery and authenticity. Willingness and determination can be our greatest asset in times of creative doubt or discouragement. It can take great courage to let go of what is familiar in order to pursue something greater. It can be difficult for an experienced artist to let go of preconceived positions. But, our next level of artistic mastery is always found *beyond* what we currently know, and beyond our past experience. With willingness, we can transform and transcend what may be limiting our creativity. When faced with creative challenges, the willingness to learn and grow can takes us from where we are now, to our next level of artistic ability.

Regardless of what we know, or *think* that we know, about what it takes to create better work, it all hangs on one decision: Are we willing, or are we not willing? "To be, or not to be, that is the question..." ponders young Hamlet in Shakespeare's play. And so it is when an artist is faced with a Creative Obstacle. A *lack of willingness* to acknowledge or overcome a creative difficulty, for whatever reason, becomes in itself a creative block. It makes no difference what we know, who we are, or what visions we have, if we are not *willing* to do the inner and outer work required to create our best and most authentic art.

Once the artist is *willing* to acknowledge a Creative Obstacle, even if it's uncomfortable, they can begin the process of transforming that obstacle and reclaim their creative energy. Sometimes, being willing to transcend a Creative Obstacle can be a matter of exploration, and sometimes a matter of real courage. There are so many ways to avoid our creative fears and challenges - drugs, food, alcohol, entertainment, shopping, busy work, distraction, and a million ways of lying to ourselves. Once we *start* the process of facing the challenges that stand in our way, our willingness can turn into creative determination.

So, what might interfere with an artist's willingness to improve their current artistic ability? There are so many possibilities - some known, and some perhaps unknown. Some people might be settled in complacency, or comfortable with the way things have always been. There may be a fear of losing an identity or public image. There may be a fear of looking like a fool, fear of being judged, or a fear of the unknown. We may be in the grips of a Secret Agenda. It may be a lack of self-esteem, self-confidence, or self-importance. Whatever the underlying reason for a lack of willingness, the Tools for the Artist in PART III can encourage creators to find enthusiasm and excitement about doing their best creative work. Taking one little step at a time can be a good start for overcoming inertia. Developing the determination and *willingness* to create our best and most authentic work, regardless of the situation at hand, is a skill worth mastering for any creative person.

"I got just one life in a world that keeps pushing me around. But I'll stand my ground, and I won't back down."

Musician and songwriter, Tom Petty

Skill #4. THE ART OF PAYING ATTENTION

What does "paying attention" have to do with being a creative genius? Plenty, my friend. Whether we prefer the term *observation*, *being present*, or *paying attention,* where you place your attention has a big influence on the quality of your work. The *source* of your creative genius will always be communicating *right here* and *right now*, so it's best to pay attention. When we are not paying attention, there is so much that we might miss. In the film, *Michael*, an archangel was asked about his psychic powers - he simply replied, "I pay attention."

But we are usually paying attention to *something,* right? It is paying attention to creating our best work right here and right now that empowers the artist. Our inner Master Artist is not a dead or stagnant thing inside of us - it is always moving, always growing, and always evolving - so If we expect to keep up, we must *pay attention* in order to move with it. Creative Mastery is not a fixed state of mind, and does not create in the past or the future. If we want to create in our "Master Artist zone," and perceive the Inspiration at hand, we listen to what is currently present even if writing about some future life on Mars.

If the voice of our creative genius started to speak, would we hear it? If Inspiration whispered in our ear, would we notice? Or would our attention be elsewhere? To make art beyond our current ability, we must set aside past stories, future scenarios, non-stop media, and what we already *think we know* in order to *pay attention* to the infinite possibilities available in the present moment.

Many artists create using elements or stories from the past, inspiration from history, possibilities about the future, and the rich world of the imagination. But we don't abandon our inner creative genius to live in those imaginary places. We use those elements to create in the present moment, where our inner Master Artist and creative genius actually live.

If *being present* holds such potential riches for a creative person, why would we resist *paying attention?* The imaginary world can often seem easier or more glamorous than this one. An artist may have creative challenges that they fear addressing. A creative person may have a "to-do" list that that they would like to avoid. It can be easy to become addicted to news, media, or entertainment. There may be uncomfortable memories or worries haunting the studio. Being distracted is one way of avoiding doubts about one's creative ability. The best way to stop any such issue from interfering with an artist's ability to stay present, is to first *acknowledge* the issue. Once acknowledged, that Creative Obstacle can be transformed, freeing the artist to be more present with their inner source on genius.

When, for example, we turn off the morning news and listen to silence, all kind of things might come to our awareness. The dream we had last night, the taste of the coffee, and the mockingbird singing outside the window. When we teach ourselves to be more observant, we discover more about the subtleties of both the outer world, and our inner life. We might find that we are actually smarter, more interesting, and more fortunate than we thought we were.

For artists, an important result of listening and paying attention is the strengthening of our powers of observation. When we are truly observing, we are able to bypass many preconceived notions. The very air around us is vibrating. Colors have endless variations. Sounds and voices reveal nuances. Our inner genius whispers in our ear when we are present. We start to see connections and mysteries that were once hidden. Artists who paint outside *en plein air,* or with a live model, discover after hours of observation that the world is more complex and mysterious than they once imagined. Artists who meditate hear things not noticed during normal life.

Anyone researching the notebooks of Leonardo da Vinci can see that he was curious enough to pay very close attention pretty much all the time. So much of what people call "genius" is simply a matter of someone being curious enough to pay closer attention.

If being present or paying attention does not come naturally, how does an artist develop this skill? Even in a busy and distracting world, it is a skill that can be learned. Here are a few practices that might help:

- Meditation is mostly paying attention inwardly. Some meditation techniques recommend watching the repetition of one's their breath going in and out. Sometimes there is a sound or mantra to focus on. Following the breath, chanting a sound, or simple listening, can help us to be more aware of the present.

- If we spend a few minutes a day writing about our observations, and even what we are grateful for, it can help us to notice more, appreciate more, and pay more attention.

- Truth is empowering, but not always easy. You can practice paying attention to what is true with meditation, tai chi, yoga, asking yourself questions, or some other practice that encourages focus.

- Painting outside with a live landscape or with a live model (rather than a photo), greatly increases the power of observation because of the focus required – it forces the artist to be present.

- You can write down recurring thoughts, concerns, or things to remember in order to get them out of your mind, and help keep your focus on your creative work.

- It helps to practice truly listening to other people when they are speaking, avoiding the temptation to speak or interject. Be present with the people (and other creatures) in your life.

- I have often set the timer on my watch to go off once every hour or so to remind myself to stop, listen, and observe. This also helps with letting go of habitual thinking patterns.

- When walking, try asking yourself questions about what you are noticing, and answer what is true in the moment.

- There are jokes told about people who talk to themselves - but it is actually a good way to be very honest and present with yourself, and a good exercise in observation.

All of these suggestions sound so simple, and they are - but very effective for increasing an artist's ability to pay attention. And paying attention can awaken us to a world of creativity. Like following the "Trail of Truth," small observations in the moment can lead to more profound ones. When paying attention, it becomes easier to bypass habitual reactions so that we make more clear and authentic creative choices. Teaching ourselves to *pay attention* increases our ability to listen to our heart, our inner genius, and our inner Master Artist.

> "Recognize what is in your sight, and that which is hidden from you will become plain to you. For there is nothing that is hidden which will not become manifest."
>
> From the Nag Hammadi Library, Thomas 5

Skill #5. THE IMPORTANCE OF MOVEMENT

One important quality of creative mastery is *movement*. Our bodies are alive and designed to move. The stars and planets are spinning and the whole universe is in a constant state of movement - even atoms and particles are in a constant state of movement. Our inner Master Artist is not standing still either – it is in a continual state of growth, expansion, exploration, and movement. Creativity itself requires action - and is never stagnant. Michelangelo wrote, "I am always learning." In order to co-create with our inner Master Artist, we must be willing to move - both *inwardly* and *outwardly* - in order to keep up with where it is going, and what it is capable of creating.

What does it *mean* to move both *inwardly* and *outwardly*? Outwardly, we move our bodies - hopefully in a way that makes us happy - to stay healthy, rid ourselves of toxins, and keep blood flowing to our brains. We work at our craft, and stretch to improve our skills. Inwardly, we explore, expand our awareness, expand our hearts, and learn new things to keep our minds vital and alive. An artist's curiosity and desire to learn keeps us in a state of movement. Outwardly, we travel to new and foreign territories to broaden our life experience. Inwardly, we expand our capacity for love, kindness, happiness, and enthusiasm for our creative work. We can spend quality time traveling in our inner universe through meditation to gain a greater awareness of our inner creative gifts.

As artists, we soon begin to realize the connection between our *inner* and *outer* movement. To be in the process of creating is to be truly alive, rather than a trained monkey, a mere product of our environment, or a simple a consumer of things. Transcendence is movement. Creation requires movement. When we transform or transcend a creative difficulty, we *move* from one state of being to a more creative state of being. Inertia, stagnation, and rigidity, regardless of justification, will most likely never contribute to your creative ability.

Running, hiking, dancing, and taking long walks can not only help us stay healthy and get oxygen into the brain, they can also move our *inner* energy. Sometimes, our creative blocks can be tied up in fixed positions or emotions that we hold in our bodies. Physical exertion, especially when it's enjoyable, makes it easier to let go of our fixed positions and gain a new perspective. I'm not sure how this works, only that it does. An active body makes it easier to feel confident, energetic, optimistic, and bring the best version of ourselves to our creative work.

When artists learn, explore, or gain a new ability, they are growing and moving. As we are learning something new in our outer world, we expand and evolve in our inner world. We transcend the old version of our self and move into a new self with more experience and more mastery. This can be learning a new language, studying with a master artist, going on a spiritual retreat, or traveling to a foreign land. Our creations come from inside of us. The art that we create shows whatever movement and expansion that we have gone through, without even trying.

"He who travels far will often see things far removed from what he believed was Truth."

Hermann Hesse, *Journey to the East*

Skill #6. PRACTICE YOUR CRAFT

One of the best ways to keep the door open to your source of Inspiration is to regularly practice and improve the skills required for our creative work. When not experiencing a lot of Inspiration, motivation, or enthusiasm, it's a good idea to keep your skills strong, or even learn new ones. When we keep our skills and work ethic strong, we are better prepared to do our best work once we begin a creative project that is important to us. If we avoid our creative work because "things are not yet just right," the inertia that we are practicing can lead to more resistance. It is during the time *between* periods of Inspiration that we continue to practice in order to keep our skills strong, and keep our creative muscles in good shape. Often, it is when we are "just practicing" that Inspiration and new ideas can drop in on us.

It helps to remember that just doing "practice work" is valuable for the artist, and is not a waste of time. It's good to take time to experiment. Not everything is meant to be a masterpiece or a source of profit. Artists benefit from doing work just for the sake of exploration, experimentation, learning, or even just for fun. When in a transitional period with no Inspiration in sight, it can be beneficial for the artist to "assign" themselves some practice work simply for the sake of exploration and keeping their craftsmanship strong. Self-assigned practice work could be a screenplay about a squirrel, a bunch of stoneware bowls for the animal shelter, filling a watercolor book with portraits of friends... Anything that keeps you working, growing, and having fun can keep your skills strong, and help to guard against discouragement. Great work often grows out of the compost of old work and failed experiments.

Some creative people may avoid practicing their skills as a means of avoiding their Creative Obstacles. But it is when we are actually working on our art form that we have the opportunity to *transform* our creative blocks and limitations. When a Creative Obstacle becomes obvious, it presents a golden opportunity to turn it around and reclaim our trapped creative energy. When practicing our craft, any creative difficulty that we come across can be acknowledged and transformed using the Tools for the Artist in the following chapters.

Time spent on travel, adventure, learning new skills, and doing important life maintenance is necessary, and can be as important to our creative work as practicing our skills. It is when we use a lack of Inspiration as a reason to avoid our work that a determination to practice becomes important. We also protect ourselves against inertia, doubts, fears, negative thinking, and other manifestations of withheld creative energy when we regularly practice our craft.

Of course, when we *are* Inspired and motivated, nobody needs to tell us to get to work. And it's hard to take the time out to practice or learn new skills when we are in the middle of an important creative project. It is when we feel completely devoid of motivation that we benefit from some self-assigned lessons or practice work - and our practice ultimately does serve our more important work, even if we feel that nothing important is happening. When the new idea, inspiration, or commission comes along, practice will keep us strong and better able to do our best work.

> "Improvisation is not the word…Make yourself available to what is being born… the undefined."
>
> Italian filmmaker, Federico Fellini

Skill #7. FIND YOUR ENTHUSIASM

Enthusiasm has its own genius, its own grace. When creative people have enthusiasm for a project, they can somehow run faster, jump higher, work longer, and spout Inspiration like a fountain. Whether sculpting marble or baking a cake, we create our best work when creating with the rarified energy of pure enthusiasm.

The enthusiasm that that we are talking about is more than a temporary excitement or the motivation to get something done. Coming from our True Self, true enthusiasm is enduring and enables us to create with an elevated ability and vision. As the enduring quality of enthusiasm is so connected to our True Self, it can remain hidden from us when we are operating out of a false, conditioned, or reactive state of mind. As an artist becomes more familiar with their True Self and what it wants to create, enthusiasm naturally starts to surface. Oddly, artists are rarely enthusiastic about projects that are completely safe, familiar, or predictable. But enthusiasm often blossoms when starting a new, challenging, or seemingly impossible creative project.

The origin of the word *enthusiasm* means "God's energy." It is a positive, motivating, and energizing force, and a natural state of our inner Master Artist. When a creative person is riding on a wave of pure enthusiasm, the whole universe seems to magically step up and help with what they are creating. Problems begin to lose their importance. Coincidences start to happen. Messages come from unusual places, and needed materials might magically become available.

For example, an artist friend had a recurring enthusiasm for learning to speak Italian... but, it seemed so senseless or impractical that they dismissed the desire year after year, even though they kept watching the same Italian movies over and over. Once they decided to investigate the unexplainable enthusiasm for the sound of Italian words, they signed up for an Italian class at the local college - inspiring even more enthusiasm. There was an unexpected joy in being in a class full of other people who also wanted to learn everything Italian. Of course, the artist wound up living and painting in Tuscany within a year. (True story)

So, how does an artist either find, or cultivate, enthusiasm when it is not already present? Chances are that if you are reading this manual for artists, you have already experienced some level of enthusiasm for creating something, at some point in life. For many artists, true enthusiasm seems to come and go of its own accord. We are excited, active, and optimistic when it is present. We experience self-betrayal when we stop short of where our enthusiasm might lead us. Without a doubt, our enthusiasm is an energy that can lead us into a state of grace, beyond our current way of creating.

Simply put, the more we *pay attention* to what we truly and consistently love - regardless of how impossible or inconvenient - the more we encourage enthusiasm. Pay attention to what you love and, and what makes you feel more alive. The dreams that we had in our youth are often a clue. Enthusiasm has a mysterious connection to the truth - meaning that once we start to deceive ourselves about what we really want to create, it can dissipate. Sometimes we need to go on an adventure, away from our familiar surroundings, in order to reconnect with the source of our enthusiasm. Even if we love our life, time in a different environment can help us to escape our familiar identity long enough to listen more deeply to what we most want to create. Both the artist's Secret Journal, and True Self/False Self Game in the Tools for the Artist section, are very effective for uncovering hidden enthusiasm. If you have an area of ongoing love, curiosity, or excitement about something, it may be pointing the way to art for which you have a great and enduring enthusiasm.

"After all, the object is not to "make art," but to be in the wonderful state which makes art inevitable."

Painter and teacher, Robert Henri, *The Art Spirit*, 1923

Skill #8. A HEALTHY SENSE OF HUMOR

For an artist, one of the best things about having a sense of humor is that it can automatically lessen the severity of our creative challenges. It helps us to not take things so personally. Humor can help us to see problems from a higher perspective and provide different points of view. Many of life's fears and difficulties eventually become funny stories. We can learn to apply that same sense of humor to our current creative limitations, as well. A sense of humor can help us to see our creative challenges in a way that is easier to face and turn around. Humor can also help artists to be less concerned about the opinions or judgments of other people.

But, using humor to unnecessarily belittle, harm, embarrass, or hurt another person is a misuse of creative energy. Playing the bully in this way can be an easy trap to fall into, especially for young people, and is often a reflection of self judgement. Paradoxically, it can be very healing for society to satirize and make jokes about tyrants who have created great harm in the world. Each individual must decide if their humor is being used for good or ill.

Humor can save one from embarrassment: On a long morning walk on a deserted beach, I saw a huge odd-looking creature swimming in the waves. Amazed by what I saw, I flagged down the first park ranger I could find, and they called for more park rangers. As the rangers were all wearing their park uniforms, and I was in a bathing suit, they asked me to take their camera out into the water to photograph the strange animal. The "creature" actually turned out to be a pod of manatees in mating season - common in inland waters, but very rare in the open ocean. They were so tightly knit that they *did* look like a sea monster. Laughing and surrounded by park rangers, I eventually looked down and realized that I was not wearing my black bathing suit at all - I had left the house wearing only black underwear. It was like that horrible kind of dream, except that it was really, really happening. All I can say is my sense of humor and the kindness of others saved me, turning what could have been a horrible experience into a laughable one. Thankfully, the park rangers still wave hello on the morning walks.

Even if a sense of humor doesn't come naturally, it is helpful for creative people to work on developing one. I truly wish that I knew how to teach others to have a Sense of Humor, because I know how valuable it is to a creative person. The song, Judy Blue Eyes says that "Fear is the lock, and laughter is the key to your heart." Watching funny movies, joking with friends, reading Far Side cartoons, or laughing at comedians can exercise our Sense of Humor. Many master artists throughout history definitely seemed to have one - humor makes the life as a creative person a lot easier. Anyone observing the animal kingdom can see that if there is a "Great Creator in the sky," whether using creation or evolution, they have a bizarre sense of humor. Having humor about our work, about our creative process, about our challenges, and especially about ourselves can add joy to our life and our creative work.

> "Father forgive us for what we must do,
>
> you forgive us, and we'll forgive you.
>
> We'll forgive each other till we both turn blue.
>
> Then we'll whistle and go fishing in Heaven."
>
> Songwriter and musician, John Prine, *Fish and Whistle*.

Skill #9. THE ARTIST'S STUDIO

As artists trying to create our best and most authentic work, we need a private place that is free from the limitations, disturbances, and distractions of life. Master Artists and Craftsmen need an environment where they have the freedom to follow their inner voice, their inner Master Artist, and hear Inspiration when it speaks.

The environment where we do our creative work can have a profound effect on our state of mind, and thus a profound effect on our art. You should feel uplifted, at home, and excited when you walk in your studio or work space. If not, then you may have some work to do. Sometimes turning an uncomfortable studio into a supportive work space is a matter of small but important changes - like music, light, smell, or organization. Or you may need to make big changes in order to create a supportive space to do your best work.

Not all artists practice their craft within the confines of one space. Even traveling performers, street artists, and tightrope walkers still need a place for planning, research, and listening to their own inner creative voice. A studio does not have to be perfect. Even if it is just a neighbor's garage or the corner of a room blocked off by a barrier of book shelves, every artist needs a place that is "their own." You need a place where nothing is compromised - free from outside opinions, disturbances, and unwanted influence.

Whether you are a painter, sculptor, architect, writer, musician, or other creator, support your inner artist by creating a studio or work area that serves you well. The outside world offers plenty of creative obstacles and limitations: World events. Media noise. Jealousies. Needy people. Well-meaning friends. Dogs who want to play. Demanding cats. Psychic influences… the list is endless. As important as it is to maintain connections to life and loved ones, artists need a place where we can hear the voice of our creative genius when it speaks to us. We need a sanctuary where we can transcend regular life and find our inner Master Artist.

> "The painter must be solitary… For if you are alone you are completely yourself, but if you are accompanied by a single companion, you are half yourself."
>
> Painter, engineer, and inventor, Leonardo da Vinci, 15 C.

Skill #10. YOUR GUIDING STAR

An artist's "Guiding Star" is a little different than the artist statements that are often required by art galleries or exhibitions. Your Guiding Star is like a personal intention or mission statement that reminds you of who you are as an artist when life gets complicated. The purpose of creating your own Guiding Star is to evoke your inner Master Artist, not to explain yourself to other people. Your Guiding Star should be in your own words, and remind you of your truest, highest, and best intention for your creative work - even if you are still discovering what that is.

We may not always be sure of what to say about the kind of work that we most want to create. That's OK. For most artists, their Guiding

Star or mission statement will evolve over time as they learn more about the nature of their True Self – even if you start with "I'll do my best." We all grow and change. The very nature of the Master Artist is growth, movement, and transcendence. The more we get to know the True Self and our inner Master Artist, the more confident we become about our creative intentions.

Don't try to compose a Guiding Star statement when feeling confused, uncertain, or uninspired. Wait until you feel enthusiastic, powerful, connected to your True Self, and able to see clearly what is most true for you in your heart.

A well-crafted Guiding Star should bring you back to a state of clarity and enthusiasm when feeling distracted or discouraged. It is best to distill your Guiding Star down into one powerful statement, rather than a long description of qualities. The words don't have to be fancy, as long as they really mean something to you as an artist. Keeping your intention short and easy to recall will make it easier to remember when needed, for example:

"I am a weightless flying Goddess when I dance."

"My films heal mankind by creating more laughter in the world."

"My work is an adventurous journey to discover who I am."

Actually, the above examples sound pretty boring because I just made them up as examples. They lack the magic, power, and authentic meaning that a true Guiding Star would have. I keep my own Guiding Star private, and it remains quite effective for me. In order for a Guiding Star to be most effective for you, it needs to be from *your own* inner voice, and not a statement found in a book, or created by somebody else. Start with something that will be meaningful to you when faced with self doubt or creative challenges. Ideally, an Inspired Guiding Star will come from your own inner Master Artist, and will resound with a motivating "ring of truth" whenever you say the words to yourself.

Creative teams working together can also benefit from having a common Guiding Star for a particular project. For a chef's kitchen, a film crew, or an educational organization, a team Guiding Star can help to keep everyone's energy working together in the same direction with cooperation and enthusiasm. With everyone working towards the same vision, Inspiration and creative genius can come from a variety of sources, rather than just the leader. There is often a unique and surprising spark of creativity that that can appear when a group of artists work together towards the same vision.

For an artist, the world can be a complicated and demanding place. We may be exposed to so much information that it starts to influence our creative decisions. We may feel tempted to make our work conform to current trends in order to fit in, or to become more marketable. In tough times, a good Guiding Star can remind us of our highest truth, what we really want to create, and restore our unique sense of direction.

For Master Artists to access their inner creative genius, they often let go of what is familiar for a while. They might let go of what the rest of the world is doing in order to create work that is new, authentic, and extraordinary. A well-crafted Guiding Star can be your friend and protector when traveling alone into "new creative territory." During times of self doubt, a good Guiding Star can help to restore enthusiasm and creative courage. We can also double check our creative choices by asking if they are in alignment with our Guiding Star. An artist's sense of security can travel with them when exploring new territory. If you lose your sense of direction, your Guiding Star can tell you what you need to hear.

"O for a muse of fire to ascend the highest heavens of invention."

Playwright, William Shakespeare, *Henry V* 1:1

"Portrait of Nikolas Krater" (detail) 1528, by Hans Holbein the Younger. Oil on wood panel, 32"x 26" Musee du Louvre, Paris, France.

19

An Introduction to the
TOOLS FOR THE ARTIST:
10 Techniques for Transforming Creative Obstacles

The following **Tools for the Artist** were specifically designed to transform creative blocks, limitations, and other challenges into a greater level of creative ability. These exercises have proven to be consistently effective for creative people, and they have stood the test of time. I encourage you to experiment with them. They can be used by artists working at any level of experience, and applied to any art form. Whether you want to transform a particular creative challenge – or - are ready to take your creative ability to a new level, these Tools for the Artist are designed to serve an artist throughout their career.

Where did these transformational exercises for artists come from? As explained in the Introduction, the Tools for the Artist evolved out of a lifelong passion for finding the source of Inspiration and creative mastery. In looking for that illusive source, I found it necessary to overcome just about every kind of creative fear, block, challenge, and limitation imaginable. After years of determination, experimentation, and documentation, these ten Tools for the Artist have been consistently effective for transforming the energy of creative challenges into the energy of creative mastery, authenticity, and enthusiasm.

When an artist decides to "up their game" and search for a more authentic and meaningful expression in their work, they might naturally face a variety of challenges. These 10 Tools can help the artist to not only meet those challenges, but actually gain insight, Inspiration, and a greater level of creative mastery in the process - *if* the artist is willing.

The Tools for Artist include:

- **The True Self/False Self Game**
- **The Art of Forgiveness**
- **Writing for Clarity**
- **The Circle Game**
- **Sound and Frequency**
- **The Art of Reading Reflections**
- **The Art of Letting Go**
- **The Art of Meditation**
- **Questioning for Clarity**
- **The Trail of Truth**

Although some of these exercises may sound quite simple, they are very effective for overcoming Creative Obstacles. Please read the instructions for each Tool carefully - you may find that they are not quite what you thought they would be. You are encouraged to try each one. Each artist and creative person is unique, and their creative issues can vary widely. Thus, it is impossible to match a particular creative challenge to a particular Tool for the Artist at any particular time. Each Tool can address a variety of blocks, challenges, or limitations. It is up to the individual artist to define their own Creative Obstacles, and to experiment with the Tools to find what is most effective for them at this time. Learning the art of transforming and transcending creative challenges has always been a part of becoming a Master Artist.

A creative person certainly does not have to be suffering with a big creative issue in order to benefit from using the Tools for the Artist. We can be happy creators, and still want to grow, learn, and experience more Inspiration. When using these Tools, a kind of alchemy can happen in the studio. The inner Master Artist has the power to transmute the most ordinary creative issues into greater ability and authenticity for the artist.

Learning to use each of these Tools can be an art form in itself. And each one can be taken to new levels and deeper meaning as you evolve as an artist. Some may be useful now, and others may be more useful ten years from now.

Spirit, God, Angels, Buddha, the Light, the Christ energy, your inner Master Artist, or any Higher Power can be invited to assist you in using the Tools for the Artist in a way that is for your "Highest Good." If you don't relate to this kind of spiritual assistance, you can simply intend for your "Highest Good" to take place anyway, as an intention.

The Tools for the Artist are for anyone, creating anything, at any experience level. You might be a student who is just beginning life in a creative field, or you might be a famous artist at the top of your game - wherever you are in your life as an artist, there is always room to grow, evolve, and share more of your inner gifts with the world. I am certainly still growing and learning. My dream is to look at the paintings on my easel and ask: "If I were older, wiser, and ten times more talented than I am now, what would be different?" and when the dream comes true, the answer will be, "Absolutely nothing."

PLEASE REMEMBER: When using the Tools for the Artist, people can gain quite a bit of awareness about the creative process. Please do not use any new awareness, or any *Master Artist Within* material, to judge, analyze, or act unkindly towards yourself or other people. The Tools are intended to be used by artists in a personal and private way. They are not meant to be used to "fix" anyone else. Remember to always be kind, respectful, and compassionate towards yourself and others.

"Originality cannot be preconceived, and any effort to coddle it is to preconceive it, and thereby destroy it." Robert Henri, *The Art Spirit, 1923*

"Portrait of William Shakespeare" by an unknown artist, c. 1600 – 1610. Oil on canvas, 22" x 17" National Portrait Gallery, London, England

20

THE TRUE SELF / FALSE SELF GAME

The True Self/False Self Game is best explained as an ongoing exercise to help the artist create with more mastery and authenticity. This game looks deceptively simple, but it can be more challenging than one might imagine. Although there is definitely a skill to playing this game, anyone can start it at any time.

Authentic and original creations come from the artist's True Self, rather than the false, invented, or conditioned aspects of the personality. So, with a better understanding of the True Self, it becomes easier to create more authentically, rather than according world's influences. The True Self/False Self Game is one of the best Tools for increasing an artist's ability to create unique, authentic, and original work.

Even if you already consider yourself to be very familiar with your True Self, you could be surprised by the results of playing this game. I was surprised after my first experience. The adventurous parts of me that sometimes got me into trouble actually turned out to be important aspects of my True Self. Parts of me that were occasionally a self-righteous-know-it-all turned out to be aspects of my False Self. As this exercise takes the artist *beyond* what they currently know about how they create, there are bound to be surprises. Playing the True Self/False Self Game is empowering for the artist looking for a deeper sense of authenticity in their work – taking them beyond what they think they know about their inner artist and their source of Inspiration.

A common creative block, or difficulty, happens when a creative person has conflicting desires, thoughts, concerns, or ideas when trying to work. The world can be a complicated place, and there are many influences - some known, some unknown. We were all born innocent, and then educated by years if information, programming, and conditioning. After a lifetime of information, coming up with an original thought can be rare - until we get to know our True Self. The insights that we gain when playing the True Self/False Self Game for a period of time can help us to tell the difference between what we have been led to believe is possible, and what we are actually capable of creating.

It's important to note that the terms *True Self* and *False Self* are <u>simple metaphors</u> for a wide variety of qualities and influences that artists create with. The name "False Self" is not meant to be degrading in any way, and is not meant to be a judgement on any part of our personality. The term mainly represents the parts of us that have been taught, conditioned, invented, intimidated, influenced, or otherwise affected. The whole point is to discover the most enduring and timeless parts of yourself so that you can create work that is enduring and timeless. The intention of the exercise is to gain a greater awareness of your inner True Self, as that is where your enthusiasm, creative genius, and original ideas come from.

Although the True Self/False Self Game seems easy to follow, it can be very challenging to stick to the rules. And <u>the rules must be followed</u> to be most effective. We might be tempted to start listing everything that we know, or *think* that we know, about our True Self or False Self. But in order to go *beyond* what we think we know, we must be careful to list <u>only a new awareness,</u> writing it down only when that new awareness happens. Immediately recording a new awareness in your journal helps to avoid the temptation to edit or rethink the new awareness. Be honest and trust yourself. Play the game.

Again, this exercise takes place over a period of time in order to paint a clear picture of your True Self. It takes time for new revelations to present themselves. Remember that the intention of the game is to go *beyond what you already know, or think you know,* about the nature of your most authentic self. What was true last year may not be so true now. Learning to create at a greater level of genius, mastery, or originality often requires us to *transcend* our preconceived notions. Transcending old beliefs or perceptions can take time. Please read and follow the instructions carefully:

INSTRUCTIONS FOR THE TRUE SELF/FALSE SELF GAME:

1. On a page in the back of your very private Secret Journal or Sketchbook, draw a line down the middle of the page. Label the top of one column "True Self," and the top of the other column "False Self." There is an example of these columns at the end of this chapter. Stick to just two columns on the page. Do not write anything else in the columns at this time. You can put a tag or bookmark on your TS/FS page in your journal in order to find it easily when needed. Again, keeping the Secret Journal very private can give you greater freedom to be as honest as possible, as you might wind up writing some pretty bizarre things over the next few weeks. You might want to place a blessing on your True Self/False Self Game, or ask for spiritual assistance if you like.

2. <u>Do not</u> begin writing a list of already known qualities of the True Self or the False Self. The columns are for <u>new awareness or revelations only,</u> to be recorded *in the moment* that you get that new awareness. This is to avoid a natural temptation to edit or over-think your entry. When you have a genuine new revelation about either your True or False Self, write it down, day or night, wherever you are - even if you have to get out of the shower. Again, the idea is to go *beyond* what you already know, and new revelations can be as fleeting as a dream. So, if your Secret Journal is not with you, write the new revelation or awareness on anything available, and then record it in the proper column later *without changing a thing*. Don't worry about how slowly the columns fill up. The columns do not have to have an even number of entries. Remember to resist the temptation to write down what you *think* you know. This game is "won" by holding out for *new* revelations that take us *beyond* our current or preconceived opinions - even if the new awareness is a quality that you have discovered in the past.

3. Keep listing entries on the TS/FS page, as they occur to you, for at least 4 weeks. Ideally, the game would go on for one year. You could have a new awareness in the middle of a conversation, watching a movie, while driving, in the studio, meditating, or anytime, anywhere. The qualities of either Self could be something it thinks, says, or does. It could be what it chooses to wear, the friends it likes, or an opinion about anything. Be as honest as you can. Be patient. Remember your sense of humor. Some of the column entries could really surprise you. If the page fills up, start on a new page with new columns. *Don't go looking for a new awareness*, because then the mind, and its opinions, will come into play. New truths seem to occur to us when least expected. Remember to avoid the temptation to write down qualities that you *assume* are accurate.

4. At the end of the 4 weeks or more, a "snapshot" of your True Self will begin to come into focus like film in a darkroom. A more objective picture of the False Self will also become clearer. When reading over the list of random entries that were recorded over time, you might be surprised by what you see. Becoming more familiar with the True Self is empowering, and our creative work will naturally become more true and authentic. The list of revelations about your True Self, developed over time, will create a picture of how it *looks* and *feels* to create in an authentic and original way. With greater clarity, we can choose with more confidence where to place our loyalty, which inner voice to listen to, and how to invest our time in studio. Becoming more anchored in our True Self also can protect us from confusion, self doubt, and a concern about the opinion of others. Above all, have kindness and compassion for yourself and others. Have fun playing the game.

"I have already settled it for myself, so flattery and criticism go down the same drain, and I am quite free."

American Painter, Georgia O'Keeffe

The Master Artist Within

True Self	False Self

An example of a True Self / False Self Game in an artist's Secret Journal:

TS	FS
Ok with down time	forgets where my real power comes from
Love working on a big project	feel pressured to get things accomplished
Bizarre sense of Humor	worried
Happy for no reason	Always in a hurry, pressed for time
Listening to Van Morrison	believes outside things will make me happy
Love a good story	wants to "fix" the whole world - now
I see beauty in the most unexpected places.	worry about what people think
GENEROUS	thoughts of revenge or justice
· good shoes ·	
happy around kids!	Does stupid things for love or attention
Beautiful comfortable clothes	Irritated
Creates thru Grace	time is not my friend
inspired to paint	fearful
Adventurous confident	Discount inspiration when it comes at an inconvenient time...
Love riding trains in Europe drinking wine	mean + petty
Kind & caring	resentful
Happy learning new things, making new things, going to new Places	Impatient
	judgemental or self righteous
Innately Loving	

NOTES

"The "Three Graces" detail of "Primavera" c.1480 by Sandro Botticelli. Tempera on wood panel, 80" x 124" Galleria degli Uffizi, Florence, Italy.

21

THE ART OF FORGIVENESS

The Art of Forgiveness is one of the most effective and immediate methods for transforming a Creative Obstacle into creative freedom. It may seem like Forgiveness would be irrelevant or unnecessary for many creative issues - but oddly, it often works for those situations, as well. The *willingness* to Forgive the source of a creative issue is such a powerful tool because it can, and does, change the world in which we live and create.

If someone or something in life has caused us harm, the memory *continues* to have power over us for as long as we hold on to our feelings, thoughts, and judgements about the experience. As all art begins within the artist, such experiences can influence our creative work - even when we don't see the connection. The Art of Forgiveness is the art of *reclaiming* our creative power, regardless of our life experience.

When does the artist use the Art of Forgiveness to transform a creative difficulty? Anytime that our state of mind is burdened by a judgment, opinion, regret, concern, limitation, doubt, fear, anger, or unpleasant memory is a good time to use the Art of Forgiveness. Anytime that we feel trapped, stupid, inadequate, persecuted, untalented, or otherwise bad about our self or our work, spontaneous Forgiveness can start to untie the knots. The Art of Forgiveness is always available when we feel afraid, confused, or don't know where to start. It's usually not an actual situation or experience that negatively influences our creative ability, but rather our *feelings* or *judgements* about them. We can practice the Art of Forgiveness until the chains are cut, and we reclaim our creative energy.

How, exactly, do we practice the Art of Forgiveness in order to transform a Creative Obstacle? No special tools or situation are required.

When faced with an issue that interferes with your creative work, you can simply start by saying, (either out loud or silently), something like:

"I completely forgive _____, and all things connected to _____."

"I forgive myself for judging _____."

"I forgive myself for wasting my time and energy on hating _____."

"I forgive God for allowing _____ to happen."

"I forgive myself for not being able to forgive _____."

"I forgive the paint for not doing what I want it to do…"

To transform a creative issue, continue to make the statements of Forgiveness, wherever they may lead you. Sometimes we follow a "trail of forgiveness" into new areas in a free-form fashion and discover more underlying issues. Practicing an intense session of Forgiveness can be particularly effective if done while running, walking, or moving the body in some way in order to help "shake off" any old energy.

Forgiveness statements do not even have to make sense, as long as we are sincere in forgiving whatever appears. Sometimes, things that we wind up Forgiving act as *metaphors* for issues that we can't quite define. Finding just the right words can often be the key to free ourselves of the creative challenge at hand. If we feel unable to Forgive something, then we Forgive *even our inability to Forgive*. We don't back down - we keep going until we feel the burden start to lift.

After practicing a few minutes of Forgiveness, people often start to feel a sense of relief in their body, or a lift in their mood. Many people say a prayer or ask for spiritual guidance and assistance when practicing the Art of Forgiveness. You can also ask all parts of your inner self to forgive any unknown, forgotten, or unconscious creative issues.

UNTYING THE KNOTS THAT BIND US

We call this exercise the "Art" of Forgiveness for a good reason. Artists can be very creative and complicated creatures. Our universe is vast and complicated. Some complicated things happen in life. Thus, the creative issues at hand may be multi-layered, multi-faceted, and multi-dimensional. So, it might take some pretty in-depth and skillfully worded Forgiveness statements to completely free the artist from certain issues. In order to transform the energy of a creatively constructed block, we often need creatively constructed words of Forgiveness to untangle the knots that bind us. In an improvisational way, we can address each bothersome feeling or thought that invades the studio with this Tool. For the Art of Forgiveness to be most effective, be as *sincere and thorough* as possible when Forgiving yourself, others, life, situations, memories, the gods, your muse, or inner issues.

3 THINGS TO REMEMBER ABOUT FORGIVENESS

- Forgiveness is a creative act that unburdens the artist and empowers them to transcend into new levels of creative ability.

- To be effective, Forgiveness statements do not always have to make sense, as long as they are sincere and thorough.

- Forgiveness does not imply agreement or approval with anything that has happened - we do it to free ourselves of the bonds that tie us to past events, people, or inner issues.

How will the artist *know* when practicing Forgiveness has been successful? Usually, we *feel* different. We may laugh or breathe a sigh of relief. We may feel more at peace. We may feel more enthusiasm for our work. There may be a greater sense of freedom or gratitude. We could simply feel more comfortable in our skin. When something or someone has truly been forgiven, there is almost always a sensation of "lightness."

And as all art begins within the artist, this new freedom will naturally show in our creative work.

Forgiving something, or someone, or even our self, does not mean that a "bad experience" is OK with us. It does not mean that we agree with anything that has happened. It does not mean that we no longer want to improve something. It does not mean that we agree to be around abusive people. Forgiveness means that *regardless* of reason, blame, or justification, we make a *creative choice* to free ourselves from the issue's control - reclaiming our valuable creative energy. Master Artists, as a creative act, can decide that no opinion, no person, no judgment, no experience, and no hard feelings will hold power over us, or over our creative work. The power of Forgiveness is the power to free ourselves and our art.

In terms of frequency or energy, *judgments* and *artistic mastery* are at opposite ends of the spectrum. Thus, our judgments (even well-founded ones) can function as creative limitations. But even when we intellectually know how disempowering it is to hold on to judgments, assumptions, or unhappy memories, it is not always easy to let go of them.

For example, imagine a sculptor in his studio trying to create new work. He remembers that at age 10 he was punched in the stomach by a schoolyard bully, and he is still occasionally haunted by the memory. At times, his imagination and creativity can turn to fantasies of revenge, righteousness, and getting justice. He still feels defensive in certain situations. Against his will, the unresolved experience influences his creative process. His work becomes imbued with feelings of being a victim. It is the sculptor who is burdened by this memory, not the bully of long ago. His creative energy is being influenced by an experience that no longer exists. But, the sculptor has a secret weapon - the Art of Forgiveness. He makes a Master Artist's decision to forgive it all. Once he starts to forgive everything and everyone connected to the memory, he ceases to be a victim. The liberated sculptor then reclaims his creative energy - empowering both the artist and his work in the studio. The artist and his sculpture start to radiate with a confident and triumphant energy.

TRICKY SITUATIONS

The tricky thing is that some judgments, assumptions, and prejudices can be very good at disguising their true nature. The artist needs to pay very close attention when inner thoughts or feelings are creating a "disturbance in the force." Forgiveness can be applied to any difficulty that presents itself, whether it makes sense or not. It is not important to understand everything - what is important is the artist's ability to *reclaim and redirect* their creative energy.

We may have a good reason or justification for holding on to issues like hate, contempt, anger, resentment, prejudice, defensiveness, and other feelings. It's human nature. We may think that these feelings protect us from further harm or injustice. But honestly, *such feelings only burden the artist experiencing them,* regardless of how justified. To unburden your creativity, cut them loose and Forgive it all.

We may have been severely mistreated. We may have been deceived or betrayed. We may have "proof" that God has let us down. World leaders may be making a mess of things. Our tribe may have been persecuted to no end. We may have been born with an affliction, or stuck with the worst family in the world... But, *regardless* of how justified or righteous our judgments, they still pollute our *inner world* and block us from our creative genius. The Master Artist forgives, and will let go of, *absolutely everything* to gain freedom from the psychic control of life's injustice. Regardless of how much another "deserves" to be judged, for your own sake, and the for the benefit of your art, *forgive them anyway.*

We may find that we are not willing to sacrifice certain judgments or memories because they somehow provide a type of "benefit." Our self-image, our relationships, or our sense of purpose may be so intertwined with our judgments that we fear losing our identity or purpose if we forgive them. The Art of Forgiveness empowers and liberates the artist to become more of their True Self – and - the True Self holds a far greater sense of purpose and identity than righteousness.

One of the most important and difficult areas to forgive is the artist's own self-doubt and self-judgment. Being an artist often requires going into unknown inner territory, exploring aspects of our inner world that the average person may not see. Creative people may do more "soul searching" because doing original and authentic work depends on it. Thus, we may find more things to question about ourselves. Deep introspection can even make us feel a bit crazy at times. When this happens, Forgiveness can be an artist's best friend. It is important to have a determination to Forgive absolutely anything and everything, even into our deepest feelings or memories, and reclaim our lost creative energy.

    The Art of Forgiveness is a practice worth mastering for any artist or creative person wanting to do their best work. Spontaneous Forgiveness requires no tools or special situations. It can be practiced anytime, anywhere, and with no preparation. It can be done out loud or silently, alone or in the company of others. Driving is a good time to practice the Art of Forgiveness. Some Creative Obstacles can be dissolved with only one or two statements of Forgiveness. Others may require some patience and several efforts, according to our ability and willingness to let go. Remember that practicing Forgiveness is a *creative act* that allows the artist to evolve into new levels of creative ability.

"The preacher said all my sins is washed away, including that Piggly Wiggly I knocked over in Yazoo…"

From the Cohen Brothers' film, *"Oh, Brother, Where Art Thou?"*

NOTES

"Dreams of the Sea" (detail) 1921, by N.C. Wyeth, American artist and illustrator. Oil on canvas, 38" x 32" Cover illustration for a 1922 Ladies Home Journal Magazine.

22

WRITING FOR CLARITY

For artists and creative people wanting to access their inner creative genius, writing can a very powerful and effective tool - even if you are not a writer. Many creative geniuses throughout history have used journals, sketchbooks, and letters to explore their inner journey, unburden their hearts, document their discoveries, and open the door to hidden worlds of creativity.

There are several forms of writing that can greatly benefit the artist. Writing might take the form of stories, journal entries, lessons learned, dreams to remember. Artists write to find a deeper meaning, clear a troubled mind, or mend a broken heart. Writing is a way that we tell ourselves the truth that often gets overlooked by mere thinking or fantasizing. There is a whole universe inside of each person that goes beyond what the world has taught us. When taking the time to tell our self the truth in writing, it can open the door to our inner genius, inspiration, and original ideas.

If you are working on a creative project and find yourself distracted by recurring thoughts, writing is a way to free yourself of unproductive thinking. If you are feeling too stuck, blocked, or otherwise distracted to do your creative work, writing can help you to dig deeper. If you are in a state of confusion that is sabotaging your work, writing can bring clarity. Brilliant ideas can appear and disappear so quickly, and writing can help you to capture those moments. Whether you are a musician, designer, sculptor, inventor, painter, or script writer, writing for your own clarity can help you to stay connected to your inner Master Artist, and the authenticity will show in your work.

Journal Writing, or writing in your sketchbook is a daily practice that can be like a friend that "checks in" with you to see to how you're doing. Telling yourself the truth in the privacy of your Secret Journal (Chapter 4) can keep you connected to your True Self, and your creative work will naturally become more authentic and interesting. In the Secret Journal, we can keep track of images we love, music we love, colors that we love, artists we love, and words we love. Writing about things that we love can reveal clues to our True Self and our inner world, So write them down.

Writing letters to people either living or dead, whether you know them or not, can be an effective way to get unresolved issues off your chest and out of your mind. Unresolved issues with other people can tie up a lot of an artist's energy. You can write a letter to anyone, and tell them absolutely anything, and then *burn the letter!* This helps the artist to reclaim any creative energy that was tied up in an unresolved issue, and redirect it into their work. It also feels good to write *thank you* notes to people, even for simple things - it creates more happiness and good will in the world when others feel appreciated. In a digital age, I love it when I get real letters with real hand writing from friends and family.

THE WRITING FOR CLARITY EXERCISE

Writing for Clarity is the practice of writing for the specific purpose of transforming a creative block, limitation, or other Creative Obstacle. As a lot of inner disturbance can be released during this exercise, <u>this type of writing should always be burned as soon as you are finished.</u>

There have been many teachers who have recommended writing exercises for clearing the mind. One of my favorites is Natalie Goldberg's "First Thoughts" exercise in her book, *Writing Down the Bones.* I love that she said, "You must be a great warrior when you contact first thoughts and write from them." Another is Julia Cameron's "Morning Pages" exercise, which has been useful for many people. A group of doctors in Spain discovered that when patients ripped up and discarded pages after writing down their thoughts and concerns, that their thoughts were then mentally discarded, as well. As a child, I actually invented my own writing exercise as a way to say things that little girls were not allowed to say out loud. In school, I unloaded my frustrations by writing one word on top of another with a fat pencil, creating an illegible black blob that kept me out of trouble with the grown-ups. One of the most powerful examples is perhaps the "Free Form Writing" exercise in the book, *Spiritual Warrior: The Art of Spiritual Living* by John Roger.

    This Writing for Clarity exercise is designed to specifically address Creative Obstacles in a more immediate fashion. This is my Tool of choice when feeling lost, overwhelmed, or really stuck during a creative project. The purpose of the exercise is to transform disturbances that can interfere with an artist's creative work or production. At the same time, unexpected ideas, insights, and answers can surface, as well. When practicing the Writing for Clarity exercise, it is best to write by hand on paper that can be burned, and not on a computer or other device.

    Like all of the Tools in *The Master Artist Within*, this one can be approached as an art form that improves with practice. Unlike some writing exercises, anything written during this Writing for Clarity exercise <u>should not</u> be read when finished. The pages are to be burned, or otherwise destroyed, at the end of the exercise. Knowing this can give the artist more freedom and courage to "clean out their inner studio" by unloading absolutely any thoughts, feelings, or concerns that come to mind. The contents of the pages are intended to be gone forever when the exercise is over, enabling the artist to create with a greater sense of inner freedom.

It is important to follow the instructions very carefully. You will need:

- A quiet and private place where you will not be disturbed.

- A period of time when you will not be disturbed.

- A stack of paper, and several pens that can take some abuse. (never a computer or other device)

- A safe candle and matches, if you like.

- A timer or stopwatch.

- A pre-designated safe place to burn your pages, like a fireplace or a metal trash can with a lid.

INSTRUCTIONS FOR THE WRITING FOR CLARITY EXERCISE:

1. Turn off your phone, computer, and other devices. Lock your door and let others know that you are not to be disturbed, if necessary. Choose a comfortable place to write. Use the bathroom before you begin, and perhaps have a glass of water with you. A box of tissues might be handy. It is best to give yourself the opportunity to write undisturbed for as long as you wish. Before you start, prepare a safe place where your pages will be burned so that it is ready at the end of your exercise. I use a small metal trash can with a tight lid. Decide on of the length of time for your exercise. You may want to try writing for 30 minutes the first time, and increase your time as you wish. Setting a timer will enable you to forget about the clock while writing.

2. If you like, you can ask for spiritual assistance, and intend for your "Highest Good" to take place. Remind yourself that everything that you write is going into the fire, so no one will ever see what you write. You are free to dump whatever presents itself out onto the paper as you write. The point is to get everything out of your head and onto the paper. This is a healing exercise, and Spirit will know your intention. So even if you write outrageous things, remember that the spirit of love and forgiveness is on your side - you won't be punished, and nobody is going to hell.

3. If there is a particular creative difficulty that you would like to overcome, you can write your request, or intention, down on a piece of paper before you begin. Then let it go and add it to the pile of paper to be burned. It's best to let go of all expectations, as well.

4. Begin by writing whatever comes into your mind, without editing, whether it makes sense or not. Write exactly what is present, without thinking about it. What you write may come out in full sentences, or it could be random words. The language may change, and your handwriting may change. Spelling, grammar, and penmanship do not matter. Being logical does not matter. Whatever happens, just keep writing.

5. If you feel stuck, just write the truth of whatever is present in your consciousness. Even if it is just "This is stupid, I have nothing to say, I'm bored, I'll keep writing about nothing just because…" Just keep writing. If things get scary, upsetting, or otherwise difficult, just keep pouring the disturbance out of your head and onto the paper. You may find yourself bearing down with the pen quite hard at times. If you cry, just keep writing. If you laugh, just keep writing. If you feel foolish, just keep writing. Remember that the intent of the exercise is to release as much as possible out onto the paper that will be burned. Some things that you write may not even belong to you - but just random words from somewhere. Pieces of a movie seen as a child, long forgotten memories, overheard conversations, things that other people did, comic book characters, and all kinds of nonsense could just show up in a Writing for Clarity session. Don't edit yourself. Just keep writing.

6. Sometimes, very important, Inspirational, or beautiful things come out of the writing sessions. I have seen unbelievably wonderful and unexpected things emerge while practicing Writing for Clarity. If this happens, you can write down the passages that you would like to keep on a separate piece of paper and set it to the side for safe keeping. Then you can go back to writing until your predesignated time is up. If the bell goes off, and you would like to keep writing, that is fine, also.

7. Your writing session is over when either the bell on your timer rings, or, you know that you are finished based on an overwhelming sense of well-being. When you are done, take your pile of writing to your predesignated burning place. Remember to never look at what you have written, regardless of the temptation - consider yourself free. Be grateful that it is gone. Light a match, set the paper on fire, and give thanks for whatever healing, grace, or clarity has resulted from your writing session. Thank yourself for your willingness and endurance. Even if you feel light headed, make sure that the fire burns safely, and make sure that the ashes are wet or cold before leaving them. Remember to blow out your candle.

"Everybody's looking for something… we don't have to look anywhere - it's right there within ourselves."

Musician, George Harrison at a Los Angeles press conference, 1974

NOTES

"Maiden, Mother, and Elder" (detail) Watercolor on paper by German artist and illustrator, Sulamith Wolfing, 1901 – 1989.

23

THE CIRCLE GAME

Sometimes artists wish for a quick way to sort out issues or competing directions while in the middle of a creative project. The Circle Game is a great Tool to use in such a situation. It can be played anywhere by drawing the diagram on paper, a cafe napkin, or a handy blank canvas. If a bit of inner confusion is the only thing standing between you and a new level of creative mastery, then try playing The Circle Game.

Simply put, The Circle Game can provide an immediate overview of how the artist's energy is being used in the studio. On lines in the drawing, we get to state what is most true for us concerning how we are using, or could use, our creative energy. The intent of The Circle Game is to help the artist to sort out conflicting motivations so that the inner Master Artist can come forward. This exercise is called a "game" because it's best to experiment and have fun with it, and to encourage a sense of humor when doing the exercise.

When we are creating with enthusiasm and a clear direction, we naturally have an abundance of energy to put into our creative work. If we find our energy, clarity, and enthusiasm fading in the middle of a project, The Circle Game can help us to unite our energies and bring more joy, clarity, and determination back into our work.

Where did The Circle Game come from? It first appeared to me during meditation when I was struggling with a loss of direction in the middle of a large series of paintings. I experimented with the diagram that I saw inwardly, and it helped tremendously. Over the years, it hasn't changed much, and it's still one of my favorite Tools. I have found it most effective to draw The Circle Game by hand in order to get all aspects of my consciousness involved in the process. There is something about the connection of mind-to-hand-to-paper that encourages one's "highest truth" to come forward. I find it especially effective for bringing more clarity, confidence, and enthusiasm into a particular creative project.

It doesn't matter how large or small your creative project is. Whether working on a new piece of art, a chapter in a book, a new vegetable garden, or an upcoming show, playing The Circle Game is bound to bring more clarity. It's best to avoid being attached to any particular outcome during this exercise, as preconceived ideas can block Inspiration or new ideas. For the duration of the game, you may want to "let go" and allow anything to happen - just in case good ideas or unexpected answers come from *beyond* the realm of normal logic. Ideas, direction, and inspiration can surface when playing The Circle Game. – so, make sure that you record any new revelations in your Secret Journal.

DIRECTIONS FOR THE CIRCLE GAME

1. Draw a small human figure in the center of a large piece of paper - a simple stick figure is just fine. Draw a circle around the figure. There is an example of how to draw a Circle Game diagram at the end of the Chapter. The little figure in the center is you. When I draw one, I like to put a heart in the center of the figure and a star over my head. This reminds me of my intent to bring love, light, and Inspiration into my work. You can write your creative project's name at the top of the paper to help keep the Circle Game "on track" with the subject at hand. You can ask for the Light, spiritual assistance, or guidance before starting, if you like.

2. Next, draw lines that radiate out from the figure to the edges of the page. Start with about eight lines, remembering that you can add more when needed. You will be writing on these lines, so give yourself as much room as possible. You can also use large paper or a chalkboard if needed. When you start writing, it does not need to be in any special order. Don't worry about how to begin, you can start with small details and see where it leads you.

3. The <u>inside of the circle,</u> with you in the center, represents how your inner Master Artist would create. On these lines inside of the circle, write aspects of how your inner Master Artist would approach this project. Write details of how you really want to be creating. Write about decisions you would make if you were creating at your best, and anything were possible. How do you create when full of purpose, confidence, and enthusiasm? What you write in your inner circle could be as simple as "happy," or as specific as "change the main character's name." You might write what it would look like, feel like, or act like to create this project with a new level of artistic mastery. Try to write insights that are alive to you in the present moment, rather than a preconceived list of qualities. This is to help "open the door" to going *beyond* what you currently know. In the Game, assume anything is possible. Try to pay close attention to what your inner guidance is saying in the moment, being as honest as possible.

4. The <u>outside of the circle</u> represents how we create when pressured, scattered, distracted, worried, conflicted, influenced, or otherwise off-track when working on our creative project. On the lines that stretch outside of the circle, write what it looks like, feels like, how you think, or how you act when you are creating as "less than your best." How do you create when trying to please others, burdened by an agenda, or over compensating for something? Be kind, but truthful with yourself. The qualities that you write outside of the circle could be as simple as "sloppy" or as specific as "compromising myself to please that group of people." Be as bold and honest as you can, and remember your sense of humor.

5. When both the inner and outer circles are full, stop and observe what you have written. The <u>inner circle</u> should reveal a "snapshot" of what it looks and feels like to be doing your best and most authentic work. In the <u>outer circle</u>, you can clearly see what it is like to create when burdened by the distractions that interfere with your work. This should be a picture of how you would prefer *not* to create. Seeing this "cartoon version" of how your inner Master Artist would approach this creative project can help you to go back to work with more clarity and direction.

"So if your whole body is full of Light. And no part of it in darkness, you will be radiant, as though a lamp were shining on you."

Luke 11:36

The Circle Game

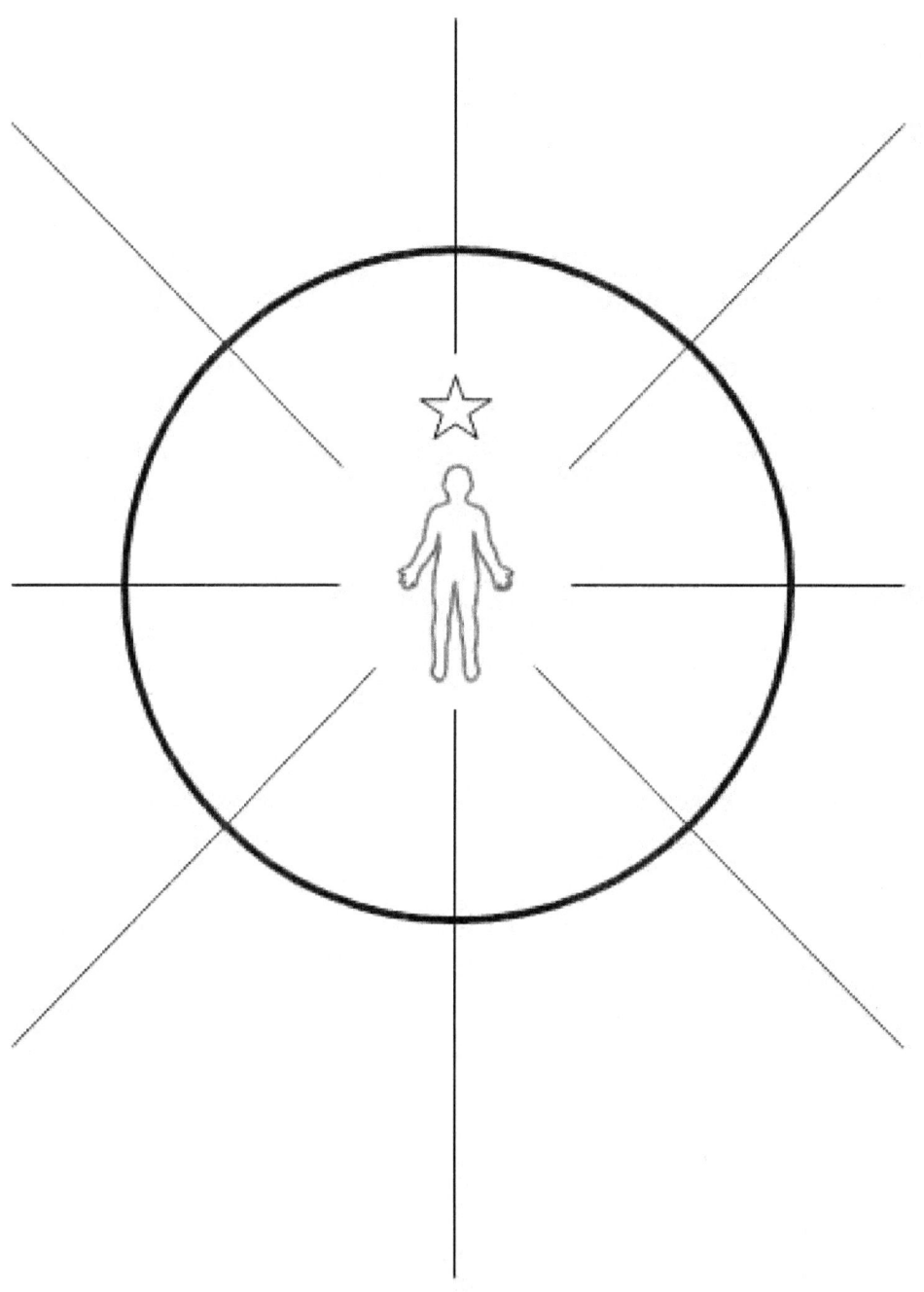

An example of a Circle Game session drawn in an artist's Secret Journal:

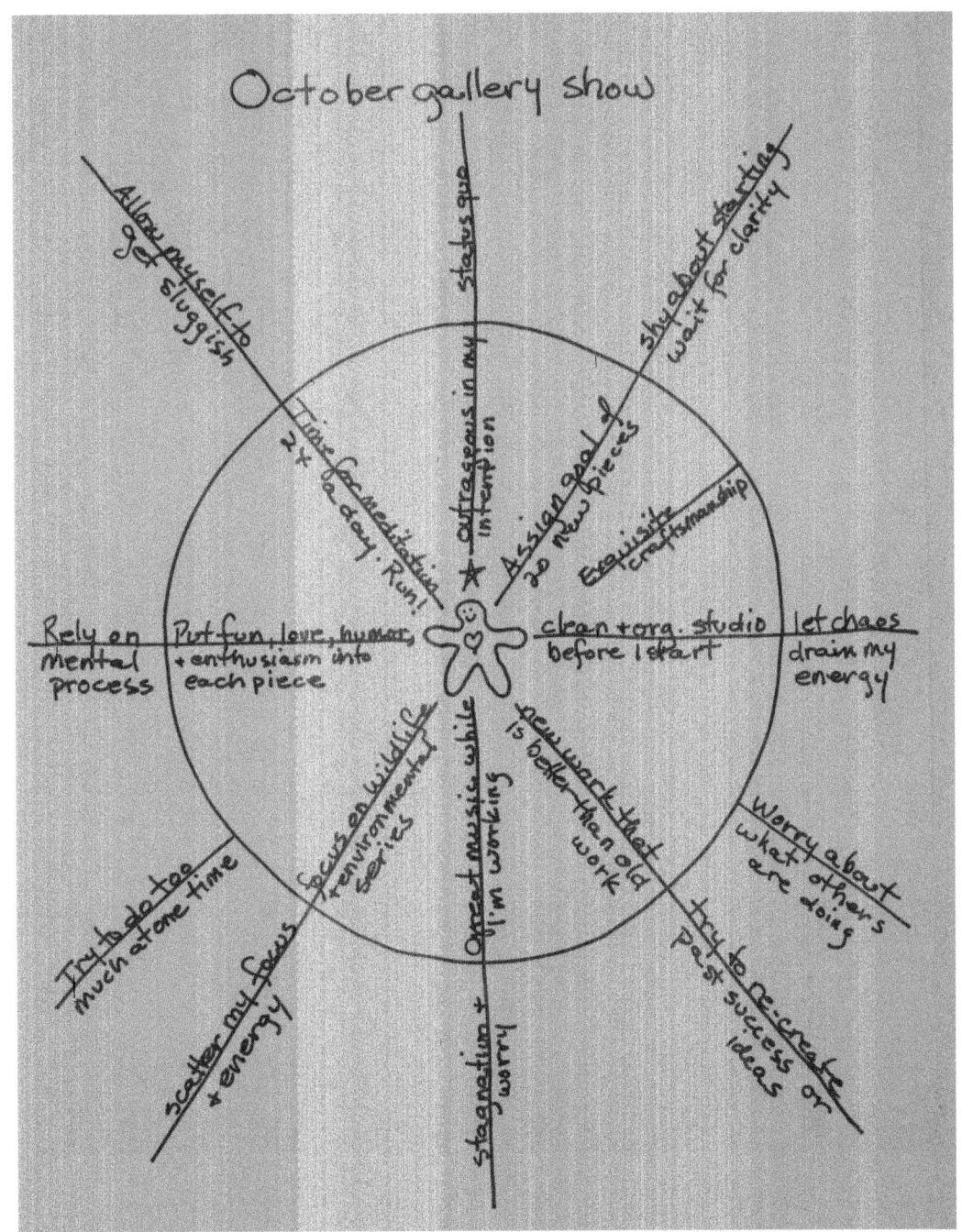

"School's Out!" (detail) by Teri Tompkins. Oil on canvas, 30" x 40"

24

SOUND AND FREQUENCY

For most artists, paying attention to the sound that we listen to on a daily basis - whether *outer* sounds or *inner* sound - can be a way to encourage a greater level of creative mastery. Without a doubt, few things in life have a more powerful effect on a person's state of mind than the sounds they hear. The whole universe, and everything in it, is vibrating at different frequencies all the time - from lower vibrations to extremely high ones. Part of creative mastery is paying attention to the sounds and words that we choose to have around us.

Different states of being vibrate at different frequencies - this is how lie detector tests and muscle testing work. As our creative work comes from us, the frequency of our state of being influences the quality of our work. So, if we are challenged by a Creative Obstacle, we can transform it by changing our inner state of being.

How does an artist use sound as a way to transform creative difficulties? First of all, we pay attention to which music, sounds, words, or frequencies have a positive effect on our state of mind and our creative work. Using sound and music is often a very effective way to lift ourselves out of a "lower frequency" of inertia or doubt and into the "higher frequency" of confidence and enthusiasm. Sound can be used to remind us of who we are.

The music that we love while driving, dancing, or socializing may not be the best music for doing our creative work. Creating is usually a different state of mind than other aspects of life. It's best to pay attention to how sound can either distract or inspire us in the studio.

The right sound can make our bodies start to dance, even when we are tired. The right song can lift our mood even if feeling depressed. Artists are multidimensional creatures, capable of a wide variety of thoughts, feeling, attitudes, and awareness. A happy song, a nostalgic song, an inspiring song, or a love song can change an artist's outlook and how they create very quickly. Whether it is a bird singing, the rhythm of a drum, or music that sweeps one away into a different reality, the frequency of certain sounds can be an artist's best friend when Inspiration and motivation are lacking.

People and animals alike use sound as an important part of their creative process. Monasteries, convents, churches, and temples radiate with song, chanting, and the ringing of bells in hopes of lifting the consciousness to a higher state. Thankfully, most communities support symphonies, orchestras, opera, and children's programs to keep classical music alive in a busy and commercially motivated society. Lovers have long used music to melt the hearts of their beloveds. Whales sing their haunting songs to each other in the deepest oceans, songbirds broadcast their unique songs into the air, and coyotes call to each other through the hills and forests.

For thousands of years, people have been chanting in different languages as a way to transcend their bodies and experience higher worlds. How can the artist use the sound in prayer and meditation to *transform* a Creative Obstacle? Creative fear, blocks, challenges, and other forms of negativity rely upon data gathered from the already-created *Known World*. When we use sound to practice transcendent forms of prayer and meditation, however, we can reach into the *Unknown World* of our spirit where the Creative Obstacles cannot go. When practicing such meditation, we can bring that original and unconditioned energy into our lives, and into our art work. The unconditioned energy that we bring from the Unknown World and into this one often inspires love, humor, genius, creativity, and compassion - enabling us to bring those qualities into the studio and into our work without even trying.

As creators, we cannot underestimate the creative power of sound through our words - not only the words that we say out loud, but also the silent ones in our imagination. The sound of certain words can lift a person up or tear them apart. Words have a unique power in that can be used to control, manipulate, heal, encourage, sell, distract, harm, or Inspire. Even small children know the difference between love and bad news in the sound of a parent's voice. Either something "rings true," or it doesn't. In his beautifully written book, *The Four Agreements,* Don Miguel Ruiz explains the importance of being "impeccable" with one's words. Whether our words and their frequencies are uttered out loud, or in the privacy of our thoughts, they can have a powerful effect on the *quality* of our creative work. Many times, it's not the definition of words in any language, so much as the *frequency* and *intent* coming from the speaker that really matters. One rarely regrets kind words.

USING SOUND AND FREQUENCY TO TRANSCEND CREATIVE DIFFICULTIES:

- Make your own list of "go-to" music that will reliably lift, encourage, and Inspire you in the studio, regardless of what is happening in your inner or outer world.

- Make an effort to remove distracting, irritating, or disturbing sounds from your environment - including appliances, televisions, music, and especially loud people.

- Be mindful of the frequency of the thoughts in your mind, and the words that you say to yourself or others. Try to maintain an inner and outer verbal frequency that encourages peace, love, and enthusiasm.

- Experiment with various mantas or tones during meditation, and notice which ones have the most uplifting and transcendent effect on you and your creative work.

As artists, we can expand our ability to use sound, music, and uplifting words to transcend creative difficulties. All art begins inside of the artist. As creative people, we can take time in our day to lift our state of being and frequency in order to bring a greater authenticity to our work. As parents and teachers, we can expose our children to music that inspires creativity, intelligence, self-confidence, and a sense of wonder. And we can also be more discerning when it comes to the sound in our daily environment - especially the place where we do our creative work.

3 THINGS TO REMEMBER ABOUT SOUND

- The right sound, music, or chanting can have a transcendent ability to lift an artist's energy and state of mind when working.

- The music or sound that encourages your best work may not be the same music that you listen to at other times.

- Speaking kind words, to yourself and others, both outwardly and in your thoughts, will have a beneficial effect on your creative work.

"The human voice vibrates naturally - but in such a way - to such a degree that it all sounds beautiful - it is the nature of the voice."

Wolfgang Amadeus Mozart, from *Mozart's Letters, Mozart's Life,* written and edited by Robert Spaethling

"I have always reckoned myself among the greatest admirers of Mozart, and shall do so till the day of my death."

German composer and pianist, Ludwig van Beethoven, 1786. From Beethoven's writings in Beethoven: The Man and the Artist, 2009.

MUSIC NOTES

"Mirror of Venus" (detail) 1875, by English Pre-Raphaelite painter, Sir Edward Burne-Jones. Oil on canvas, 47" x 78" In the collection of the Calouste Gulbenkian Museum, Lisbon, Portugal.

25

THE ART OF READING REFLECTIONS

The Art of Reading Reflections is a way for the artist or creative person to "see with new eyes." We might have assumptions or preconceived ideas that can interfere with our ability to see as clearly or deeply as possible. Using reflection as a tool, the artist can gain the ability to bypass those assumptions. The ability to see with new eyes enables the artist to exercise greater mastery in their creative work by seeing and understanding what may otherwise remain hidden or disguised. Reflection offers a different perspective. Artists can learn to improve their work by using the new perspective made possible through various methods of reflection. The Art of Reading Reflections can take several forms:

MIRRORS

A simple example is Leonardo da Vinci's method of using a mirror to look at paintings in reverse in order to spot ways to make the painting even better. In the mirror image, he might see that an eye was crooked, that the perspective was off, or that a color was needed - in a way that was not obvious by looking *directly at* the painting. It is a wonderful day when we look at our work in the mirror and absolutely love what we see!

We all have preconceived ideas about what we are seeing when we create. We might draw a model with preconceived ideas how a body should look. We are so accustomed to seeing things in a certain way, that our preconceptions can override the truth of something. But seeing our art though a reflection gives us the ability to *see beyond* our familiar way of looking. We can trick our brains into being better artists by making corrections according to what we are able to see in reverse. Some artists can also "see with different eyes" by looking at their work upside down, or in photographs.

REFLECTIONS THROUGH OUR ART

As creators, it can difficult to see just how to take our work "to the next level" when we want to improve. We might look at our creative project and feel that it could be better without knowing exactly *why* or *how* it can be better. When this happens, we can objectively write down what bothers us, whether it makes sense or not. Our intent in recording what we do not like about something is to "inwardly" transform the disturbance to improve the work.

For example, I might look at my painting and write that it feels "too rigid," even if I don't understand how. Again, all art begins with the artist. If I am holding a rigid attitude about something, I might be see that rigidity being reflected back to me through my painting. Knowing that my painting came from inside of *me,* I might consider how I am being "too rigid" in my life - rigid with myself, rigid with others, rigid in my belief about something… If I do identify some rigidity in my life, I would the go to the Tools for the Artist in Part III to transform the rigidity that is affecting my work. I might practice Writing for Clarity, practice the Art of Forgiveness, or remember my Sense of Humor. I would embrace the part of me that felt the need for rigidity, and encourage it to "lighten up." The creative energy that was tied up in rigid behavior would become more relaxed, enabling me to bring more of my True Self into the painting. The creative energy that was once influenced by "rigidity" could now be directed in a more relaxed, masterful, and authentic way.

REFLECTIONS THROUGH OTHERS

A more challenging way for artists to practice the Art of Reading Reflections is by observing people or situations in our world that bother us. We often recognize a trait, behavior, image, or expression because it reminds us of something in ourselves. Is there something in a film that is a reflection of something that is true about our self? Is a person that gets on your nerves reflecting an aspect of your own life that is hard to see? Is it possible that another artist's work is irritating because it is reflecting something you would rather not see in your own work? Do you resent someone because they are doing something you wish you were doing? These questions are worth asking, as happy artists are usually not bothered by much of anything. As your art comes from *you*, hidden feelings like judgments, resentment, irritation, or contempt can act as a negative influence on your creative work. Reflections can help us to see these inner issues in a way that we may not otherwise see. We can best serve our inner artist, and our creative work, by transforming such reflected issues from within. The Art of Forgiveness, Writing for Clarity, and The Art of Letting Go can all help to transform hidden creative issues that come to light through what we see reflected around us.

REFLECTIONS OF WHAT WE LOVE

When we see works of art that we really love and feel inspired by, we are often seeing a reflection of something wonderful in ourselves. When inspired by a favorite writer, painter, composer, architect, inventor, or other master artist, we may be drawn to their work because it reflects some aspect of what we have inside of us as artists. Of all the creations throughout time, there is a reason that we become more enlivened by some works than others. Some master creators or works just seem to speak to us. If parts of who we are as a Master Artist remain hidden to us, works that we love can serve as clues as to who we are, and what we are capable of creating. Pay attention to works of art that you consistently love - they may play a part in your awakening to your inner Master Artist. Your Secret Journal is a good place to keep track of the beauty, people, music, and creations that you find inspiring, and to investigate what they may be reflecting to you about your yet-to-be-discovered inner world.

TRANSFORMATION

How do we use the Art of Reading Reflections to transform a creative block or limitation? First, we can be honest about what is being reflected to us about our inner reality - through a mirror, our work, a person, a film, or anything else. What are we seeing reflected to us about our inner world? Is it something wonderful, mysterious, or beautiful? Is it a block or limitation that we would like to transcend? Often, simple awareness can be enough to start transcending the challenge at hand, or to start expressing more of the beauty that we see.

Through the Art of Reading Reflections, we strengthen our ability to see things that we may not otherwise see. Whether we look through a mirror, or look directly at our work, or observe things that Inspire us, what we see reflected is an invitation to become better creators. The good news is that any creative challenge that we do find reflected to us can be seen as a "cache of hidden creative energy" that we can reclaim and redirect. The Art of Reading Reflections can help us to grow in creative mastery and authenticity by giving us a greater ability to understand the inner world of the artist.

"Yes, child: art is the mirror you make to reflect your invisible dreams in visible pictures. You use a glass mirror to see your face; you use works of art to see your soul."

The playwright, George Bernard Shaw, *As Far As Thought Can Reach, 1920*

NOTES

"Joseph the Carpenter" (detail) c.1642 by French painter, Georges de La Tour. Oil on canvas, 54" x 40" Musee du Louvre, Paris, France.

26

THE ART OF LETTING GO

The Art of Letting Go is the practice of sacrificing what is no longer true, useful, or inspiring, in order to upgrade to something better. There many aspects to the Art of Letting Go that are important to an artist learning to create with a greater level of mastery and authenticity.

When growing into a Master Artist, it helps to Let Go of clutter in our environment that robs us of the space we need. We can Let Go of old habits that keep us in an old state of mind. We can Let Go of toxic relationships that sabotage our creative work and choose kinder friends. We might Let Go of our old self-image as we grow more into our True Self. We may need to Let Go of an old way of working when we grow into a new level of mastery. We can wipe out the part of the painting that just isn't working, and boldly paint over it with a clearer vision.

Many cultures throughout history have practiced scary rituals involving sacrifice - as if any deity would even want an old goat. But the sacrifice that we practice in the Master Artist Within does not involve hurting anyone or throwing virgins into a volcano… The Art of Letting Go is the *good* kind of sacrifice - like trading in broken tools for strong new ones. As we discover obstacles that interfere with our ability to do our best work, we learn to let them go. We can reclaim our time, space, energy, attention, and resources - and redirect them towards doing our best work.

There are times when practicing the Art of Letting Go can be a challenge. Some things can be difficult to let go of. I have seen artists, designers, and writers who keep working over and over on something they no longer even like, simply because they have invested so much into the project that they just can't call it quits. Some creations, or life experiences, turn out to be "practice work," and it is helpful make that OK. Practice is valuable and necessary for creative mastery. We can make peace with past ideas that once seemed brilliant but did not stand the test of time. We still get to keep what we learned to strengthen and inform future work. It can be a burden to allow past ideas or creations to become "sacred cows" that drain our creative energy. To evolve in our artistic mastery and authenticity, it helps to practice the Art of Letting Go.

Many creative blocks and limitations stem from a refusal to Let Go of something - a past experience, a heartache, religious dogma, an old idea, obsolete promises, Grandmother's dishes, an old self-image, a style of writing, a superstition, judgements about something… there are so many possibilities. But when we understand that our artistic genius, mastery, and authenticity become more accessible to us when we Let Go of burdensome attachments, it becomes easier to free our creative energy.

Sometimes we are forced to Let Go of something - or someone - against our will. When a loved one dies, it can be very difficult to accept that they are gone. This type of grief takes time, and it seems there is nothing we can do about it. As this type of *letting go* of someone was decided by life, not by us; it can be hard to accept the seeming injustice of it. We just have to honor the process, follow the Trail of Truth, and keep doing our creative work until we evolve into our next stage of mastery.

When trying to complete this book, I struggled with the Art of Letting go for weeks. I was determined to finish before the "due date" in order to get back into the studio, and an exciting new body of work. (art speak for a bunch of paintings) Hurricane season was approaching, but I was confident about finishing long before conditions became serious. Suddenly, there were three storms out in the Atlantic Ocean. I kept writing, as my plans for the rest of the year depended on completing the project on time. When Irma became an official "category 5" hurricane, I reluctantly had to take a couple of days off to secure the house, get supplies, and test the generator. I looked at the calendar, looked at my remaining chapters, and tried to fool myself into believing that I could still hold on to my schedule as the sky started to darken. The electricity and internet were gone, but hey, I can write manually by candlelight - so no problem. The hurricane eventually hit my island and raged through the night. I tried to sleep on the couch to keep an eye on things. At 4:30 in the morning, a big oak tree that I had known my whole life came crashing down on the house, and through the kitchen roof. At 5 am, standing in the dark, a hot cup of coffee in my hands, rain pouring through the ceiling, I finally realized: "Dang, I might need to Let Go of the due date."

Taking more time to finish the book has actually turned out to be a very good thing. Part of creative mastery is the *willingness* to create with your *best* ability, from the *best* part of yourself, in *any* situation. Transcendence. Enthusiasm. Authenticity.

Creative mastery is unconditional - it will do its best, with what it has to work with, in the face of any challenge. Overcoming a creative challenge just produces more energy. Resistance and attachment take energy to maintain, so we exercise Letting Go when our creative mastery requires us to do so. I call this tool the "Art" of Letting Go because there is an art to knowing what, how, and when it's time to Let Go of something in order to "upgrade" and create in a better way. When we practice the Art of Letting Go, even when it's difficult, we free our creative energy to transcend into a new level of creative ability.

"And I will never grow so old again

And I will walk and talk in gardens all wet with rain…"

Sweet Thing, 1968, from the album, *Astral Weeks*, Northern Irish singer and songwriter, Van Morrison

The mysterious "Mona Lisa" or "La Joconde" 1503 – 06, by Leonardo da Vinci. Oil on wood panel, 30"x 21" Musee du Louvre, Paris, France.

27

MEDITATION AS AN ART FORM

Many artists, performers, and creators already know that Meditation is a simple practice that can make a big difference in the quality of their life and creative work. Why is Meditation such an effective Tool for creative people? Because in our mind, we can have a lot of thoughts, memories, beliefs, images, and preconceived notions about everything. And, Meditation can allow us to go *beyond* all of that. Effective Meditation can help us to transcend our Known World so that we can see things in a new, original, and more authentic way.

Regardless of all the books, products, and spiritual retreats available to teach Meditation, it can be as simple as breathing in and out, and as natural as listing to a mockingbird. It is true that the Beatles went all the way to India to study Transcendental Meditation in the 1960's. But these days, finding instruction is as easy as turning on your computer. Meditation is also a Tool that the artist can use anytime, and anywhere.

As artists, we become our own path in a way - so discovering the most powerful and effective way to Meditate for each individual is a personal matter. I am certainly not qualified to be a Meditation teacher, but after a lifetime of experience, I do know how valuable it is to an artist's creative work. Much of *The Master Artist Within* methodology came to light during periods of Meditation. The truth is that in the innocence of childhood, most humans often slip into a trance, a daydream, or some transcendent state – which I consider to be all natural forms of Meditation. It is said the Einstein got his best ideas while shaving – I would guess that it was because while shaving, his mind was allowed to wander beyond his normal logic and thought patterns.

How does an artist use Meditation to transform creative limitations? Creative Obstacles are made up of ideas, fears, beliefs, and experiences from our familiar Known World. When we Meditate, we are often lifted into a higher frequency, a higher perspective, and gain more awareness of our inner life. During Meditation, we can learn to travel in our consciousness beyond the Known World into realms where Creative Obstacles do not exist. In the Unknown World, we can get a new sense of who we are, and what we are capable of creating. When we lift into this higher perspective, many limitations that we experience naturally begin to transform or dissipate. We might lose a taste for things we once liked. We might drop habitual behaviors without even trying. We might laugh at things that we once took seriously. As our creative work originates inside of us, our art might start to radiate with a new energy.

There are many opinions about *how* to Meditate - from the casual to the highly disciplined. For the creative person who wants to awaken their inner Master Artist, is there a "most effective" form of Meditation? For pursuing Inspired creativity, I recommend Meditation with an intent to *transcend* the artist's normal life, and normal way of seeing things. The type of Meditation that I practice is of the transcendent type, as the intent is to experience other realms of consciousness beyond the material world. Some forms of Meditation focus on peace, relaxation, calming the mind, and other goals – all worthy endeavors. In my favorite yoga class, we all Meditate together while listening to Sanskrit chanting, which is wonderful. I also like to Meditate while walking, hiking, or running. There is no real mystery to Meditating, but it can open the door to greater mysteries.

One can try Meditating in a certain position, Meditating lying down, and Meditation while moving. There is silent Meditation. There are tones and mantras for Meditation. People Meditate as a form of prayer. There are group Meditations, global Meditations, and solo meditators. Meditation happens morning, noon, and night. Some meditators are initiated by Masters, and some learn how to Meditate by watching online videos. (This is starting to sound like a Cole Porter song) The important thing is to experiment, finding the form of Meditation that is most effective, enjoyable, and beneficial for you and your creative work.

Creative people are served well by taking the time to practice a Meditation that allows the consciousness to transcend the concerns of the world for just a little while. The ability to transcend our schedules, preoccupations, and inner noise - in order to simply observe and listen inside - can help us to see and create from a higher perspective. So, what do we focus on or listen to while Meditating? You can start with silence, chanting, your breath, your heartbeat, the ringing in your ears... Thoughts will come and go, and it seems the more we resist them the more they persist. Its best to just smile and let the thoughts be there. Writing for Clarity or journal writing before Meditation can help with rampant thinking. We can imagine lifting above the noise - like hiking up a mountain while the houses below fade away. It's good to keep your Secret Journal nearby for things you'd like to remember.

Each master work that was ever created was an act of transcendence. To transcend is to "go beyond." Each artist, writer, or inventor did something to *go beyond* what was already known, sometimes creating works of art with a frequency that we call "timeless." As our creative works reflect our inner state of being, the quality of our work can noticeably transform when we practice Meditation. The energy, peace, and Inspiration after periods of Meditation can help us to transcend our creative limitations, and open the door to the source of our inner genius.

As artists, how do we approach our Meditation as an art form? Like all of our skills, we find what truly works for us, what gives us the most energy, what opens our heart, and what helps us to see better. We can regularly practice and refine our Meditation skills like our other creative skills. Many artists and creative people chant a sound, a word, or a mantra to start their meditation. Anyone new to Meditation can try chanting Om, Hu, Shanti, Love, or a word or sound that is uplifting. There are plenty of examples of chanting on the internet. Ultimately, the point is go inside and experience your higher self, listen to the truth of your heart, and become aware of the different realms of your inner world.

3 THINGS TO REMEMBER ABOUT MEDITATION:

- Meditation is a beneficial tool that artists and creative teams can use anytime and anywhere, as long as they are safe.

- Meditation can help creators to transcend the limitations of fear, thoughts, feelings, images, and preconceived ideas – and does not rely on religious belief.

- There is no mystery to practicing Meditation, but it can open the door to greater mysteries.

"The energy that I've found doing meditation, you know, has been there before - only that I could access it only on good days when everything was going well. With meditation I feel that it could well be pouring down rain; it's still the same amount."

John Lennon, *The Frost Programme* interview, 1967

NOTES

"Questioner of the Sphinx," 1863, by American artist Elihu Vedder. Oil on canvas, 36" x 42" Museum of Fine Arts, Boston, Massachusetts.

28

QUESTIONING FOR CLARITY

Since the time of the early Greek philosophers, the art of inquiry has been used to evoke a greater truth and awareness. For an artist or creator, asking the right question at the right time can inspire new answers and new ideas. Sometimes, it may not even occur to us that there is a different perspective - until we are asked a question that urges a deeper look. A good question is an invitation for a new truth to come forth that was not already apparent. We might have a whole universe of wisdom, ability, and genius locked away inside of us just waiting for the right question to help us open the door.

So how can the asking of a question help an artist to create better work? How can a question help to transform a creative block or limitation? If an artist is creating with assumptions, preconceived ideas, or a set of limited beliefs, challenging those limitations with the right questions can help the artist to come up with new possibilities.

Whether dealing with a profound creative issue, or a relatively simple one, an artist can get down to the truth of an issue by asking questions. Here is a simple example of an artist questioning an unresolved creative limitation:

"I wish that I was good at drawing hands."

"How often have you tried?"

"Once or twice a year, unless I can avoid it."

"How important is it to your work?"

"Hands are very important. But I can't draw them well, so I've gotten good at avoiding them in my compositions."

"Haven't we taken a class for this?"

"Well yes, but my drawings weren't as good as the other students. It was embarrassing."

"How would you advise a child if they wanted to be able to draw hands really well?"

"I would suggest that they draw hands once a day for a whole year until it became second nature. The year will go by anyway, so why not?"

"Is there anything that you have done every day for a whole year?"

"I start every morning by making coffee, without fail."

"Is the ability to draw really beautiful hands as important to you as coffee?"

"Actually, so much more important - I have been wanting to solve this problem for years!"

"Are you willing to spend a few minutes a day for the next year to make this dream come true for yourself?"

"It never occurred to me before, but now I'm excited about taking on the challenge!"

The asking of good truth-evoking questions can awaken an artist's wisdom and remind them of why they wanted to be an artist in the first place. Some people ask themselves the same question over and over again in order to get down to a deeper level of truth about their creative intentions. All artists and creative people have innate genius and wisdom inside of them. And, asking the right question can evoke that genius and wisdom. We are often surprised by the answers and good ideas that we have hidden inside of us.

There are all kinds of questions listed at the end of this chapter. But I encourage you to create your *own* questions designed to address your personality, your art form, your unique situation, and help you to create your best and most authentic work. You can also create questions that help you to stay on track with the direction encouraged by your Guiding Star.

My favorite portrait painting teacher provides students with a list of questions to ask during the final stages of their painting in order to "quality check" the portrait, and to look for opportunities to make the work even better. You can devise your *own* series of quality check questions to ask yourself in the studio that are designed to help you to produce your most masterful, original, and authentic work.

Some of the questions below are directed towards one's *state of being* while creating. Some questions are directed towards the creative process, and how the creative energy is being directed. And other questions can be directed towards an actual work of art or creative project.

Depending on your current situation, some questions will be more relevant than others. Again, these questions are mainly to serve as examples, and meant to encourage artists to compose their own questions. Often, the most difficult questions to answer can be the most productive in transcending or transforming a creative issue.

Remember that the purpose of practicing Questioning for Clarity is to gain more creative clarity - and never to be unkind to yourself or others. The Questions can also be used simply for artistic growth, exploration, and experimentation. The important thing is to be honest with yourself, and to use the questions in a way that is most beneficial and empowering for you.

Example Questions to Ask Yourself in the Studio:

- What do I most love about my work?

- Does this work make me feel happy and alive?

- Am I doing my best with this work?

- Am I recreating something familiar or safe?

- When am I most happy, carefree, and full of energy while creating?

- What am I most enthusiastic about?

- When do I most feel like my True Self?

- Am I sharing the best of myself in this work?

- Is my heart as open, kind, and generous while working?

- How am I different from anyone who has ever existed?

- If I were 10 times a better artist, what would I do differently?

- Is there anything I need to do my best work?

- Can I make my work environment more uplifting or supportive?

- When I am old, what am I going to wish I had created?

- If I were fearless, would my work be different?

- Am I withholding something that I wish I could say, do, or create?

- If anything were possible, what would I love to create?

- Is this work a replacement for what I really want to create?

- If I were a Master Artist, how would this be different?

- If I were more confident, successful, admired, wealthy, etc., would I be doing something different?

- To what degree am I being true to myself?

- Am I allowing anything to sabotage the quality of my work?

- What am I willing to do to overcome this limitation?

- Am I supporting my creativity by taking good care of my health?

- Am I putting my love, genius, wisdom, light, or humor into this work?

- If this were my last week on earth, what would I want to do?

- If time or money were not an issue, what would I be creating?

- What is the most important thing in the world to me?

- Can I unburden myself by letting go of something?

- Is there something that I can forgive, or let go of, to improve my work?

- What would my inner Master Artist do?

- In ten years from now, what am I going to wish I had done?

- If I were totally unconcerned about the opinions of others, would anything be different?

- If I were Mozart, Shakespeare, Michelangelo, or my favorite artist, would I be working in a different way?

"At the heart and core of Lawrence of Arabia is "Who am I?"

Steven Spielberg speaking about director David Lean in the documentary, *"Spielberg"* 2017

"City of Light" 2013 by Teri Tompkins. Oil on canvas, 48" x 36"
Private collection.

CHAPTER 29

TOOLS FOR THE ARTIST: THE TRAIL OF TRUTH

Artists wanting to pursue their next level of creative mastery find that they must stretch *beyond* what they already know, and *transcend* their current level of artistic ability. And there is rarely a road map to get there. One way to stretch into Master Artist territory is to follow what I call the "Trail of Truth." Following the Trail of Truth means to *pay very close attention* to the truth as we observe it in the present moment, which allows the next truth beyond that to unfold. When we *do* pay very close attention to what is present, the small and insignificant truths lead to more important truths, and then even bigger truths beyond that, until we find ourselves seeing things or ideas that were once beyond our awareness.

Creating at our best is creating with the greatest level of truth, enthusiasm, and inventiveness that we are capable of at any given time, regardless of the situation. Sometimes this is correcting the shadow on a drawing, and sometimes it is cleaning the studio. Following the Trail of Truth requires trust, because sometimes it may be difficult to believe that the present truth will support us more than a familiar lie, pretense, imitation, or illusion. We must trust ourselves and our inner Master Artist, even when we don't know where the Trail of Truth will lead us.

We can create more authentically and find new enthusiasm if we are willing to follow the truth where it takes us. This doesn't mean doing something foolish just because we are temporarily convinced that something is true. When inspiration is lacking, or thoughts are scattered, we can track what is true and present by writing, by talking out loud, or by speaking to ourselves silently the things that are true in our heart of hearts. As simple as this sounds, once we let go of the past, future, or imaginary stories in order to acknowledge what is currently true for us, the results can be really quite surprising. Being awake, aware, and present in the moment can lead one from trivial details to more meaningful content. Mysteries can begin to unfold. Like a bloodhound following a scent, we say or write the next true thing until it takes us, and our creativity, to places we did not expect.

Following the Trail of Truth can require some courage when the present truth is uncomfortable. Whether an unpleasant thought, an unpleasant feeling, or an unpleasant chore that needs to be done, we must acknowledge it in order to go beyond it to the next level of truth. Years ago, I saw a documentary with Paul Simon giving advice to a group of African songwriters. He said something like, "There's no such thing as writer's block, you just don't want to write the next thing that wants to be said…" And I've often found that to be true. We may *not* want to put the "next thing that wants to be said" into our art, but we must say it anyway to get past it and on to the good stuff. The original idea that we *are* looking for could be hiding just beyond that "unsayable" thing. So say or write that next thing, even if it's ugly, then add it to the compost pile when no longer needed.

At times, the present truth requires acknowledging the next thing that needs to be done. In a busy world, there seems to be no end to our chores and responsibilities. Following the Trail of Truth can help us to discern the difference between what is truly important to complete, and what unnecessarily keeps us from doing our best work. Some projects don't stand the test of time. When artists try to mentally force new works of art while still in process with other work, the creative energy can be split. Often, clarity and Inspiration for the next piece of art, the next song, or the next chapter unfolds as we complete the project at hand to the best of our ability.

When we are in the studio and don't know what to do next, we can follow the Trail of Truth by doing what we *do* know. Doing what we *do* know can *lead us* to the next step, and then the next step after that. Even if the next step is doing the laundry, we still do the next step on the Trail of Truth, until clarity and Inspiration appear. As artists, inventors, writers, and creative people, we become our own path. In a world full of demands and distractions, we might feel pressured to know everything about what we are creating before we actually get there. We must respect the timing of our inner Master Artist, doing our part to take good care of what has been revealed to us in times of true Inspiration.

Some people have a habit of "unloading" their issues on others in the name of truth, claiming that they are "just being honest." This is *not* following the Trail of Truth. When I see such behavior, it is usually someone *projecting* their own self judgements and shortcomings onto a captive audience in order to feel better about themselves. It is a misdirection of creative energy to use truth or honesty as an excuse to be unkind to others. The creative person will develop more inner strength when they recognize the reflection of their own issues or opinions, transform them inwardly, and direct their valuable creative energy into doing good work.

When we follow the Trail of Truth, we let go of the assumption that we already know everything. Opinions, preconceived ideas, brainwashing, and limiting beliefs can all block us from listening to our inner creative genius when it speaks. Anyone who paints landscapes outside en plein air, or figures from live models, knows that paying attention to the truth can be very different from what we might imagine. To follow the truth, we sometimes have to ramble, to give it all up, and to say, "I don't know what the hell is going on…" Letting go of assumptions can allow us to follow our own path to our inner creative genius, and hear what it has to say.

Mythologically speaking, it often seems that creative jewels and riches are hiding in dark caves guarded by big scary dragons. Although this sounds ridiculous, many creative people miss out on much of their potential by avoiding the opportunity disguised as a creative fear, block, or other challenge. Not everyone is interested in artistic mastery or authenticity. Some prefer the comfort of a predictable and familiar world, with no wish to travel beyond the status quo. This is fine. But when we do transcend our creative challenges, we find deeper creative riches and original ideas buried within us.

So follow the Trail of Truth to where your inner Master Artist resides. Follow it to the unique source of genius that in all the universe, can only come through you. If anything gets in your way, forgive it, laugh at it, write it out, rise above it, or find a way to use it to allow your inner Master Artist to shine – creating a better world by simply being and creating as who you really are.

"Nothing is truer than truth. All mistakes committed by artists are due to their having separated themselves from truth, believing that their imagination is stronger… there is nothing stronger than nature. With nature in front of us, we can do everything well.

Spanish painter, Joaquin Sorolla y Bastida

NOTES

NOTES

References and Notes

FRONT MATTER:

- The Pieta, marble sculpture by Michelangelo Buonarroti, Italian sculptor, painter, architect, and poet, 1478-1564. Basilica di San Pietro, Vatican City, Italy

- "I have had a vision…" *A Midsummer Night's Dream* 4:1, 1595, William Shakespeare, English playwright, poet, and actor, 1564-1616.

CH 1:

- *Lives of the Most Excellent Painters, Sculptors, and Architects*, 1550, Giorgio Vasari, Italian painter, author, and historian, 1511-1574.

- "Inspiration is an awakening…" Italian opera composer, Giacomo Puccini, 1858-1924.

- *Astrophysics For People in a Hurry*, 2017, Neil deGrasse Tyson, American astrophysicist, author, and speaker.

"…even greater things…" John 14:12 New International Bible

- "The divine element in art…" The notebooks of Leonardo da Vinci

- "His Strength.." Alec Guinness quote in the film, *David Lean: A Life In Film,* 1985, (director Nigel Wattis) about David Lean, English filmmaker, 1908-1991.

CH 2:

- "There are more things…" Hamlet 1:5 by William Shakespeare. c.1600

- "I shall give to you…" Gospel of Thomas 17, from the ancient Nag Hammadi Library scrolls, found in the Egyptian desert in 1945, this translation by Thomas O. Lamdin. Coptic Museum, Cairo, Egypt. gnosis.org

CH 3:

- "There is no exercise…" *The Secret of the golden Flower: The Classical Chinese Book of Life*, 1991 translation of ancient text by Thomas Cleary.

CH 4:

- "My work has escaped…" *The Letters of J.R.R. Tolkien*, 2013, edited by Humphrey Carpenter and Christopher Tolkien. About J.R.R. Tolkien, English author, poet, professor, 1892-1973.

CH 5:

- Association of Waldorf Schools of North America, waldorfeducation.org

- "The hurt you embrace…" Jalal ad-Din Muhammed Rumi, Persian poet and mystic,1207-1273.

CH 6:

- "Do not judge…" Luke 6:37 *New International Bible*

"I would permit no man…" *Up From Slavery*, 1901, Booker T. Washington, American writer, speaker, educator, and presidential advisor, 1856-1915.

CH 7:

- "This above all…" *Hamlet* 1:3, William Shakespeare, c.1600

CH 8:

- "One must still have chaos…" *Thus Spoke Zarathustra: A Book for All and None*, 1883-91, Friedrich Nietzsche

CH 9:

- "There is something bigger…" American architect Bernard Maybeck (1862-1957), from a *Sunset Pacific Monthly* interview with Lois J. Stellmann, Vol 35 No 5, 1915, speaking about his intention for the Palace of Fine Arts in San Francisco

CH 10:

- "Like an artist with no art form…", *Sula*, 1973, Toni Morrison, American author and teacher.

CH 11:

Where to start for immediate help with addictions:

1. SAMHSA - The Substance Abuse and Mental Health Service Administration

2. U.S. National Helpline, 1-800-662-4357

samhsa.gov

Free, Confidential, 24 hours a day, 365 days a year

2. **Alcoholics Anonymous**

aa.org

3. **Narcotics Anonymous**

na.org

4. For an emergency in the USA:

call 911 or go to the nearest **Hospital Emergency Room**

- "From this hour…" *Leaves of Grass*, 1855, Walt Whitman, American poet and author, 1819-1892.

CH 12:

- "It looks sad…" from the poem, *Underwater in the Fountain*, Jalal ad-Din Muhammed Rumi.

CH 13:

"If you hear…" Vincent van Gogh, in a letter to Theo van Gogh, October 28, 1883.

CH 14:

"How he comes o'er us…" *Henry V* 1:2, William Shakespeare, 1599.

CH 15:

- "There is a vitality…" Martha Graham, from *The Life and Work of Martha Graham*, 1991,

 by Agnes de Mille, p264, about Martha Graham, American dancer and choreographer, 1894-1991.

CH 16:

- Everglades National Park, Florida   nps.gov/ever 305-242-7700

- Panic and anxiety: Reid Reichardt, SelfTherapy.org , mc2method.org

- "Obstacles cannot…" Leonardo da Vinci, from the journals of Leonardo da Vinci.

CH 17:

- "Schubert was crazy, you know…" *West Wing* episode 1999, written by Aaron Sorkin. Referencing *Ave Maria* by Franz Schubert, German composer, 1797-1828.

- "To anyone out there.." James Elder, international writer, explorer, and big wave surfer, 2017.

https://suicidepreventionlifeline.org

Lifeline: 1-800-273-8255 (USA)

Panic attacks: https://www.selftherapy.org

Your local **Hospital Emergency Room**

CH 18:

- "I realized…: from the film, *A River Runs Through It*, 1992, by Robert Redford (American actor and filmmaker). Film based on a Norman Maclean story (American writer, 1902-1990).

1. "Self love, my liege…" *Henry V*, 2:4, William Shakespeare

2. "Love many things…" Vincent van Gogh, Dutch painter, 1853-1890.

3. "I got just one life…" , from the song, *I Won't Back Down*, Tom Petty and Jeff Lynne, American musicians, songwriters, and performers.

4. "Recognize what is in…" Thomas 5, Nag Hammadi Library

Michael 1996, film directed by Nora Ephron, screenplay by Nora Ephron, Delia Ephron, Jim Quinlan and Peter Dexter.

5. "He who travels…" *Journey to the East*, 1932, Hermann Hesse, Swiss author and painter, 1887-1962.

6. "Improvisation is…" Federico Fellini in an interview.

7. "After all…", *The Art Spirit*, 1923, Robert Henri, American painter and teacher, 1865-1929.

8. "Father forgive us…" from the song, *Whistle and Fish, 1978,* by American singer and songwriter, John Prine.

"Fear is the lock…" from the song, Suite: Judy Blue Eyes, by Crosby, Stills, and Nash, 1969, written by Stephen Stills

The Far Side Galleries by American cartoonist, Gary Larson.

9. "The painter must…" Leonardo da Vinci, from the journals of Leonardo da Vinci.

10. "O for a muse…" *Henry V*, 1:1, William Shakespeare

CH 19:

- "Originality cannot…" Robert Henri, *The Art Spirit*, 1923

CH 20:

- "I have already settled…" American painter, Georgia O'Keeffe, *The Art and Life of Georgia O'Keeffe*, 1985, Jan Garden Castro.

CH 21:

- "The preacher said…" from the film, *Oh, Brother, Where Art Thou?*, 2000, by Joel and Ethan Coen, and based on Homer's Odyssey.

CH 22:

- *Spiritual Warrior: The Art of Spiritual Living*, John Roger, 1997

- *Writing Down the Bones, Freeing the Writer Within*, Natalie Goldberg, 1986

- *The Artist's Way: A Spiritual Path to Higher Creativity*, Julia Cameron, 1992

- *Psychological Science Magazine*, Brinol, Gasco', Petty, Horcajo, University of Madrid

- "Everybody's looking…" Musician George Harrison MBE in a LA Press Conference in 1974 (English singer, musician, and songwriter, 1943-20010)

CH 23:

- "So if your whole body…" Luke 11:36, *New International Bible*

CH 24:

- *The Four Agreements,* 1997, Don Miguel Ruiz, Mexican author and teacher.

- "The human voice…" Wolfgang Amadeus Mozart, *Mozart's Letters, Mozart's Life*, 2005,

edited and translated by Robert Spaethling.

- "I have always reckoned myself…" Ludwig van Beethoven, German composer and pianist, 1770-1827. About Wolfgang Amadeus Mozart, Austrian composer and musician, 1756-1791.

CH 25:

- "Yes, child: art is…" *As Far As Thought Can Reach*, 1920, Irish playwright and author, George Bernard Shaw, 1856-1950

CH 26:

- "And I will never be so old again…" from the song, Sweet Thing, Astral Weeks, 1968, Irish musician, singer, poet, songwriter, Van Morrison.

CH 27:

- "The energy that I've found…" English musician, singer, songwriter, John Lennon, (1940-1980) in an interview with David Frost, 1969.

CH 28:

- "At the heart and core…" Steven Spielberg speaking of David Lean in the HBO documentary, *Spielberg*, 2017, director Susan Lacy.

CH 29:

- "Nothing is truer…: Juaquin Sorolla y Bastida, Spanish painter, 1863-1902.

Illustration Notes

Intro: Detail of the "Pieta" sculpture by Michelangelo Buonarroti, 1498 - 1500, finished when he was about 25 years old. Carrara marble, 5.9' x 6.9.' (174 x 195cm) Basilica di San Pietro, Vatican City, Italy

Ch 1. "Self Portrait" (age 29) by Albrect Durer, 1500. Oil on panel 26.4" x 19.3" (67.1x48.9cm) Alte Pinakothek Museum, Munich, Germany

Ch 2. "Astronomer by Candlelight" (detail) by Gerrit Dou, 1650's. Oil on panel, 12 ⅝ x 8 ⅜ (32x21.2cm) Getty Museum, Los Angeles, California.

Ch 3. "Joan of Arc As Shepherdess" (detail) by Jules Eugene Lenepveu, 1889. The first of four mural panels in the Pantheon, Paris, France.

Ch 4. "Rain and Bullet" (detail) by Teri Tompkins, 1886. Watercolor on paper, 28x22, private collection.

Ch 5. "The First Maine Fishermen" (detail) by N. C. Wyeth, 1937, used as an illustration for *Trending Into Maine* by Kenneth Roberts. Oil on hardboard panel, about 35 x 25 (88.9x63.5cm), private collection.

Ch 6. "The Perfectionist" (detail) by Grant Wood, 1936. Crayon, gouache, charcoal, and ink on paper, 20" x 16", The Fine Arts Museums of San Francisco.

Ch 7. "Ophelia by the Pond" by John William Waterhouse, 1894. Oil on canvas, 49" x 29" (124.5x73.5cm) Private collection.

Ch 8. "Vertumnus" by Giuseppe Arcimboldo, c.1590. Oil on wood panel, 28" x 23". Portrait of Rudolf II, Holy Roman Empire as the Roman god, Vertumnus, in the Skokloster Castle, Sweden.

Ch 9. "Ellen Terry as Shakespeare's Lady Macbeth" by John Singer Sargent. According to a letter written to a friend, Sargent wanted to paint the actress in full costume after seeing her perform on stage. Oil on canvas, 87" x 45" (221x114.3) Tate Gallery, London, England.

Ch 10. "At Merlin's feet the wily Vivien lay" by Gustave Dore, 1860's. One of many steel engravings made to illustrate Alfred, Lord Tennyson's book of poems, *Idylls of the King*.

Ch 11. "Bacchus" by Michelangelo Mersi da Caravaggio, c.1595. Oil on canvas, 37 ½" x 33 ½" (95x85cm), Galleria degli Uffizi, Florence, Italy.

Ch 12. "The Great Wave of Kanagawa" 1830, color woodblock print, 10"x15" (25.7x37.9cm) by Katsushika Hokusai (1760-1849). Print #21 of the series, "Thirty Six Views of Mount Fuji" In the collection of the Metropolitan Museum of Art, New York, N. Y.

Ch 13. "Boreas" 1903, by John William Waterhouse. Oil on canvas, 32" x 25" (79.8x63.8cm), private collection.

Ch 14. "The Loge" by Mary Cassatt, c.1878. Oil on canvas, 31½" x 25" (79.8x63.8cm) National Gallery of Art, Washington, D.C.

Ch 15. "Carolina Parakeets" (detail) by John James Audubon, 1885. Watercolor, graphite, pastel, gouache, and ink on mounted paper, illustration The Birds of America by Audubon, 1826-38, original in the collection of the New York Historical Society. Native to the US, Carolina Parakeets are now extinct, with the last wild specimen reportedly shot in 1904.

Ch 16. "Seein' Things at Night" (detail) by Maxfield Parrish, 1903. Oil on paper, 21" x 15" (53.3x38.1cm) Painted for the book, "Poems of Childhood" by Eugene Field. Also used for the cover illustration for a 1903 Ladies Home Journal Magazine, private collection.

Ch 17. "Starry Night" (detail) by Vincent van Gogh, 1889. Oil on canvas, 29" x 36" (73.7x92.1cm), painted during his time at an asylum near Saint-Remy- de-Provence. The Museum of Modern Art, New York, N.Y.

Ch 18. "Mice Sewing the Mayor's Coat" (detail) by Beatrix Potter as an illustration for The Tailor of Gloucester, c. 1902. Watercolor on paper, Tate Gallery, London, England.

Ch 19. "Portrait of Nikolas Krater" (detail) by Hans Holbein the Younger, 1528. Oil on panel, 32 ½ x 26 ½ (83x67cm) Louvre Museum, Paris, France.

Ch 20. "Portrait of William Shakespeare" by an unknown artist, c.1600-1610. Oil on canvas, 21 ¾" x 17 ¼" (55.2x43.8cm) National Portrait Gallery, London, England.

Ch 21. The "Three Graces" detail of Sandro Botticelli's painting, "Primavera", c.1480. Tempera on wood panel, 80" x 124" (202x314cm) Uffizi Gallery, Florence, Italy.

Ch 22. "Dreams of the Sea; A Boy's Fantasy" (detail) by N.C. Wyeth, 1921. Oil on canvas, 38" x 31¾" (96.5x80.6cm) Used as the cover illustration for a 1922 cover for Ladies Home Journal Magazine.

Ch 23. "Maiden, Mother, and Crone" (detail) by Sulamith Wolfing, German artist and illustrator, 1901-1989.

Ch 24. "School's Out" (detail) by Teri Tompkins. Oil on canvas, 30 x 40, private collection.

Ch 25. "The Mirror of Venus" (detail) by English Pre-Raphaelite artist, Sir Edward Burne Jones. Oil on canvas, 42.2"x78.7" (120x200cm) Calouste Gulbenkian Museum, Lisbon, Portugal.

Ch 26. "Joseph the Carpenter" (detail) c.1642, by Georges de La Tour. Oil on canvas, 54"x40" (1.3mx1m) Louvre Museum, Paris, France.

Ch 27. "Mona Lisa" or "La Gioconda" by Leonardo da Vinci, 1503-1506. Oil on panel, 30 ¼ x 21 (77x53cm) Louvre Museum, Paris, France.

Ch 28. "Questioner of the Sphinx" by Elihu Vedder, 1863. Oil on canvas, 36¼ x 42¼, (91.44x106.68cm) Museum of Fine Arts, Boston, Massachusetts.

Ch 29. "City of Light" 2013, by Teri Tompkins Portrait of the Winged Victory of Samothrace marble sculpture in the Louvre Museum, Paris. Oil on canvas 40" x 30," private collection

Photo by Jesse Miller

Teri Tompkins is a professional artist and teacher with a doctoral degree in spiritual science, focusing on creative energy. She has lived, traveled, painted, and studied art history internationally, and now lives in her home town of St. Augustine, Florida.

TeriTompkins.com

www.ingramcontent.com/pod-product-compliance
Lightning Source LLC
Chambersburg PA
CBHW060311240426
43661CB00059B/2732